Math
Expressions
Volume 2

Developed by
The Children's Math Worlds Research Project

PROJECT DIRECTOR AND AUTHOR
Dr. Karen C. Fuson

This material is based upon work supported by the
National Science Foundation
under Grant Numbers
ESI-9816320, REC-9806020, and RED-935373.

Any opinions, findings, and conclusions, or recommendations expressed in this material
are those of the author and do not necessarily reflect the views of the National Science Foundation.

 HOUGHTON MIFFLIN HARCOURT

Teacher Reviewers

Kindergarten
Patricia Stroh Sugiyama
Wilmette, Illinois

Barbara Wahle
Evanston, Illinois

Grade 1
Sandra Budson
Newton, Massachusetts

Janet Pecci
Chicago, Illinois

Megan Rees
Chicago, Illinois

Grade 2
Molly Dunn
Danvers, Massachusetts

Agnes Lesnick
Hillside, Illinois

Rita Soto
Chicago, Illinois

Grade 3
Jane Curran
Honesdale, Pennsylvania

Sandra Tucker
Chicago, Illinois

Grade 4
Sara Stoneberg Llibre
Chicago, Illinois

Sheri Roedel
Chicago, Illinois

Grade 5
Todd Atler
Chicago, Illinois

Leah Barry
Norfolk, Massachusetts

Special Thanks

Special thanks to the many teachers, students, parents, principals, writers, researchers, and work-study students who participated in the Children's Math Worlds Research Project over the years.

Credits

Cover art: (t) © Superstock/Alamy, (b) © Steve Bloom Images/Alamy
Illustrative art: Dave Klug
Technical art: Morgan-Cain & Associates

2011 Edition
Copyright © 2009 by Houghton Mifflin Harcourt Publishing Company

Printed in the U.S.A.

ISBN: 978-0-547-47390-1

1 2 3 4 5 6 7 8 9 10   1421   19 18 17 16 15 14 13 12 11 10

4500228446   X B C D E

ii

VOLUME 2 CONTENTS

Unit 9 Fractions

Mini Unit 10 Three-Dimensional Figures

Unit 11 Decimal Numbers

Big Idea Decimal Concepts

Big Idea Comparing and Ordering

Big Idea Number Lines

Big Idea Add and Subtract Decimal Numbers

Big Idea Estimation With Decimals and Fractions

Mini Unit 12 The U.S. Customary System

Extension Lesson

Glossary

Class Activity

Name _____   **Date** _____

Vocabulary

divisor
quotient
dividend

▶ Divide Hundreds

In mathematics, special words are used to describe parts of a problem.

Discuss these multiplication and division words.

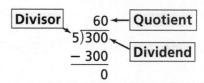

Multiplication Words

$$60 \leftarrow \boxed{\text{Factor}}$$
$$\times\ 5 \leftarrow \boxed{\text{Factor}}$$
$$\overline{300} \leftarrow \boxed{\text{Product}}$$

$$\boxed{\text{Factor}} \rightarrow 60$$
$$5\overline{)300} \leftarrow \boxed{\text{Product}}$$
$$\underline{-\ 300}$$
$$0$$

Division Words

$$\boxed{\text{Divisor}}\ \ 60 \leftarrow \boxed{\text{Quotient}}$$
$$5\overline{)300} \leftarrow \boxed{\text{Dividend}}$$
$$\underline{-\ 300}$$
$$0$$

1. Describe the relationships among these 5 words in rectangles.

_____

_____

▶ Three Division Methods

The sidewalk crew knows that the sidewalk is 330 square feet. The sidewalk is 5 feet wide. How long is the sidewalk? Ellie, José, and Wanda each use a different method to find the answer.

Ellie's Rectangle Sections Method

a.
$$5\ \boxed{330}$$

b.
$$5\ \boxed{\begin{array}{c} 60 \\ 330 \\ -\ 300 \\ \hline 30 \end{array}}$$

c.
$$5\ \boxed{\begin{array}{cc} 60\ + & \\ 330 & \\ -\ 300 & \\ \hline 30 & \end{array}}$$

d.
$$5\ \boxed{\begin{array}{cc} 60\ + & \\ 330 & 30 \\ -\ 300 & \\ \hline 30 & \end{array}}$$

e.
$$5\ \boxed{\begin{array}{cc} 60\ + & 6 \\ 330 & 30 \\ -\ 300 & -\ 30 \\ \hline 30 & \end{array}}$$

f.
$$5\ \boxed{\begin{array}{cc} 60\ + & 6 = 66 \\ 330 & 30 \\ -\ 300 & -\ 30 \\ \hline 30 & 0 \end{array}}$$

José's Expanded Notation Method

g.
$$5\overline{)330}$$

h.
$$\begin{array}{r} 60 \\ 5\overline{)330} \\ -\ 300 \end{array}$$

i.
$$\begin{array}{r} 60 \\ 5\overline{)330} \\ -\ 300 \\ \hline 30 \end{array}$$

j.
$$\begin{array}{r} 6 \\ 60 \\ 5\overline{)330} \\ -\ 300 \\ \hline 30 \end{array}$$

k.
$$\begin{array}{r} 6 \\ 60 \\ 5\overline{)330} \\ -\ 300 \\ \hline 30 \\ -\ 30 \\ \hline 0 \end{array}$$

l.
$$\begin{array}{r} 6 \\ 60\overline{)66} \\ 5\overline{)330} \\ -\ 300 \\ \hline 30 \\ -\ 30 \\ \hline 0 \end{array}$$

Class Activity

Vocabulary

remainder

▶ Three Division Methods (continued)

Wanda's Digit-by-Digit Method

m.	n.	o.	p.	q.	r.
5)330	6 5)330 − 30	6 5)330 − 30 3	6 5)330 − 30 30	66 5)330 − 30 30	66 5)330 − 30 30 − 30 0

Write the answer on a separate sheet of paper.

2. How are their methods alike?

3. How are their methods different?

4. What other methods do you know that could solve this problem?

5. How do the division methods relate to the multiplication methods below?

Rectangle Sections Method

$$
\begin{array}{c}
\quad 60 \;+\; 6 \\
5\; \boxed{\begin{array}{c|c} 5\times 60 & 5\times 6 \\ = 300 & = 30 \end{array}}
\end{array}
\qquad
\begin{array}{r}
300 \\
+\;30 \\ \hline
330
\end{array}
$$

Expanded Notation Method

$$
\begin{array}{rr}
66 = 60 & +\;6 \\
\times\;5 = & 5 \\ \hline
5\times 60 = & 300 \\
5\times\;6 = & 30 \\ \hline
& 330
\end{array}
$$

▶ Understand Remainders

We call the leftover quantity in a division problem the **remainder**. We write an "R" before a remainder.

Discuss and compare this problem.

The school store sells pencils in five-packs. The students who run the store have a box of 332 single pencils. They need to know how many five-packs can be made from the box of single pencils.

6. How are this problem and the sidewalk problem on page 279 alike, and how are they different?

Find the Unknown Factor

Name _____

Date _____

▶ Discuss Patterns in Remainders As Products Increase

Write the answer to each exercise, including any remainders.

7. 5)30   5)31   5)32   5)33   5)34   5)35

8. 5)43   5)44   5)45   5)46   5)47   5)48

9. 5)300   5)301   5)302   5)303   5)304   5)305

10. 5)354   5)355   5)356   5)357   5)358   5)359

Look for patterns in your remainders, and answer the following questions.

11. What happens to the remainder part of the quotient as the dividend increases by 1?

_____

12. What is the smallest number of single pencils the store could have and make exactly 66 five-packs?

_____

13. What other numbers of single pencils could the store have and still make 66, but not 67, five-packs?

_____

14. What numbers of single pencils could the store have and make 68, but not 69, five-packs?

_____

15. How big can a remainder be? Why?

_____

_____

_____

_____

▶ Division and Money

Suppose you and your four friends earn $55 cutting grass. It is important for you to know how to divide so that you can share the money equally.

- Divide the ten-dollar bills into 5 equal groups.

- Divide the one-dollar bills into 5 equal groups.

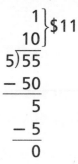

```
    1 }$11
   10
5)55
 −50
   5
  −5
   0
```

Next week, you and your friends earn $65. How should you divide the extra ten-dollar bill?

- The ten-dollar bill would have to become 10 one-dollar bills.

- Each friend would get 2 more dollars.

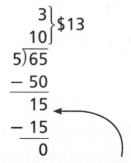

```
    3 }$13
   10
5)65
 −50
   15 ←
  −15
   0
```

Here you change one $10 for ten $1 to get $15 to share.

1. Amy earned $100 in 5 days. If she earned the same amount of money each day, how much money did she earn in one day?

_____

Show your work.

2. Chris made $250 for 5 hours of work. How much did Chris earn per hour?

_____

Dear Family,

Your child is familiar with multiplication from earlier units. Unit 7 of *Math Expressions* extends the concepts used in multiplication to teach your child division. The main goals of this unit are to:

• Learn methods for dividing whole numbers up to five digits.

• Use estimates to check the reasonableness of answers.

• Solve problems involving division and remainders.

Your child will learn and practice techniques such as the Rectangle Sections, Expanded Notation, and Digit-by-Digit methods to gain speed and accuracy in division. At first, your child will learn these methods using 5 as the divisor, as most students have little difficulty with 5 count-bys. Later, the methods are extended to divisors of 2, 3, 4, 6, 7, 8, and 9. Then your child will learn to divide when there is a zero in the quotient or dividend and to watch out for potential problems involving these situations.

Examples of Division Methods:

Your child may use whatever method he or she chooses as long as he or she can explain it. Some children like to use different methods.

Rectangle Sections Method	Expanded Notation Method	Digit-by-Digit Method

Rectangle Sections Method:

$$60 + 6 = 66$$

5	330	30
	− 300	− 30
	30	0

Expanded Notation Method:

$$
\begin{array}{r}
6 \rceil\,66 \\
60 \\
5\overline{)330} \\
-300 \\
\hline
30 \\
-30 \\
\hline
0
\end{array}
$$

Digit-by-Digit Method:

$$
\begin{array}{r}
66 \\
5\overline{)330} \\
-30 \\
\hline
30 \\
-30 \\
\hline
0
\end{array}
$$

Your child will also learn to interpret remainders in the context of the problem being solved; for example, as fractions of a whole or as decimal amounts of money.

Finally, your child will apply this knowledge to solve mixed problems with one or more steps and using all four operations.

If you have questions or problems, please contact me.

Sincerely,
Your child's teacher

Estimada familia:

En unidades anteriores su niño se ha familiarizado con la multiplicación. La Unidad 7 de *Math Expressions* amplía los conceptos usados en la multiplicación para que su niño aprenda la división. Los objetivos principales de esta unidad son:

- aprender métodos para dividir números enteros de hasta cinco dígitos.

- usar la estimación para comprobar si las respuestas son razonables.

- resolver problemas que requieran división y residuos.

Su niño aprenderá y practicará técnicas como áreas de rectángulos, notación extendida y dígito por dígito, para adquirir rapidez y precisión en la división. Al principio, su niño aprenderá estos métodos usando 5 como divisor, ya que la mayoría de los estudiantes tienen poca dificultad cuando cuentan de 5 en 5. Más adelante los métodos se extenderán al uso de los divisores 2, 3, 4, 6, 7, 8 y 9. Luego, su niño aprenderá a dividir cuando haya un cero en el cociente o en el dividendo, y a detectar problemas que pueden surgir en esas situaciones.

Ejemplos de métodos de división:

Su niño puede usar el método que elija siempre y cuando pueda explicarlo. A algunos niños les gusta usar métodos diferentes.

Método del área de rectángulos	Método de notación extendida	Método de dígito por dígito

$$
\begin{array}{r|r|r}
 & 60 \;+ & 6 = 66 \\
\hline
5\, \bigl| & 330 & 30 \\
 & -300 & -30 \\
\hline
 & 30 & 0
\end{array}
$$

$$
\begin{array}{r}
6\rceil \\
60\rceil\,66 \\
5\overline{)330} \\
-300 \\
\hline
30 \\
-30 \\
\hline
0
\end{array}
$$

$$
\begin{array}{r}
66 \\
5\overline{)330} \\
-30 \\
\hline
30 \\
-30 \\
\hline
0
\end{array}
$$

Su niño también aprenderá a interpretar los residuos en el contexto del problema que se esté resolviendo; por ejemplo, como fracciones de un entero o como cantidades decimales de dinero.

Por último, su niño aplicará este conocimiento para resolver problemas mixtos de uno o más pasos, usando las cuatro operaciones.

Si tiene alguna pregunta o comentario, por favor comuníquese conmigo.

Atentamente,
El maestro de su niño

Find the Unknown Factor

▶ Division With Four-Digit Dividends

Wanda, Ellie, and José each use their favorite method to solve 1,194 ÷ 5.

1. Discuss how their methods are alike and how they are different.

| Ellie's Rectangle Sections Method | José's Expanded Notation Method | Wanda's Digit-by-Digit Method |

Ellie's Rectangle Sections Method

```
        200  + 30  + 8 = 238 R4
   5 | 1,194 | 194 | 44 |
     | -1,000| -150| -40|
        194    44    4
```

José's Expanded Notation Method

```
        8 ⌉
       30 | 238
      200 ⌋ R4
   5)1,194
   - 1,000
      194
    - 150
       44
     - 40
        4
```

Wanda's Digit-by-Digit Method

```
      238 R4
   5)1,194
   - 1 0
      19
    - 15
      44
    - 40
       4
```

On a separate sheet of paper, rewrite each problem in long-division format. Solve, using any method.

2. 3,248 ÷ 5 = _____

3. 4,873 / 5 = _____

Find the product P for each problem.

4.   1,000
   5)‾P‾

   5 × 1,000 = P

   P = _____

5.   3,000
   5)‾P‾

   5 × 3,000 = P

   P = _____

6.   6,000
   5)‾P‾

   5 × 6,000 = P

   P = _____

7.   8,000
   5)‾P‾

   5 × 8,000 = P

   P = _____

Solve, using any method.

8. 8,435 ÷ 5 = _____

9. 18,435 ÷ 5 = _____

10. 37,265 ÷ 5 = _____

11. 44,714 / 5 = _____

Vocabulary

partial-quotients method

▶ Estimate Quotients to Solve Division

When you divide, you ask, "How many groups of a given size are there in the total amount?" With each step, you estimate and try to find the closest answer.

In the **partial-quotients method**, you make a series of estimates and then add them up at the end. This method is similar to the Expanded Notation Method, but the partial quotients are written next to the division problem instead of above it. Beginning with tens is an easy way to start.

- Start with $10 \times 8 = 80$ to solve $8 \overline{)178}$. This works, but maybe 20×8 is closer to 178.

- Try 20×8. The product of 20 and 8 is 160, which is closer to 178, so we use 20 as our partial quotient. Write 20 to the side as shown.

- Next ask, "How many 8s are in the remaining 18?"

- Write 2 to the side as shown and then subtract 16 from 18.

- Finally, add the two partial quotients, 20 and 2. The final result is this sum along with whatever was left over as the remainder.

$$
\begin{array}{r|r}
8 \overline{)178} & \\
-160 & 20 \\
\hline
18 & \\
-16 & 2 \\
\hline
2 & 22 \\
\end{array}
$$

22 R2

Solve on a separate sheet of paper. Use partial-quotients division.

1. $6 \overline{)132}$ 2. $7 \overline{)189}$ 3. $12 \overline{)157}$

4. $5 \overline{)1,035}$ 5. $8 \overline{)977}$ 6. $9 \overline{)285}$

▶ Solve Problems, Using Partial Quotients

Solve.

7. Sonja has 175 stamps in her collection. There are an equal number of stamps on each of the first 7 pages of her collector's book. How many stamps are on each page?

Class Activity

Name _____   Date _____

▶ Discuss Division Word Problems

1. A helper in the school store suggests selling notebooks in packages of 4. How many packages of 4 can be made from 192 notebooks?

_____

2. Another student suggests selling notebooks in packages of 6. How many packages of 6 notebooks can be made from 192 single notebooks?

_____

3. The store will sell packages of notebooks for $3.00 each. Would packages of 4 or packages of 6 be a better deal for students?

_____

_____

_____

_____

4. Which package size would make more money for the store?

_____

_____

_____

_____

Another helper suggests making packages of 7 or 8 notebooks and selling them for $6.00 each.

5. How many packages of 7 notebooks can be made from 192 notebooks?

_____

6. How many packages of 8 notebooks can be made from 192 notebooks?

_____

7. Would you rather buy a 7-pack or an 8-pack? Why?

_____

_____

_____

8. Would 7-packs or 8-packs make more money for the store?

_____

_____

_____

▶ Division Exercises

Use any method to solve.

9. $3\overline{)2,061}$

10. $9\overline{)432}$

11. $2\overline{)1,476}$

Name _____ **Date** _____

Going Further

▶ Mental Math

Look for patterns with zero when dividing multiples of 10 or 100 by 10.

$20 \div 10 = 2$	$200 \div 10 = 20$
$50 \div 10 = 5$	$500 \div 10 = 50$
$30 \div 10 = 3$	$300 \div 10 = 30$
$90 \div 10 = 9$	$900 \div 10 = 90$
$110 \div 10 = 11$	$1{,}100 \div 10 = 110$

$$2 \times \underset{1}{\underline{\frac{20 \div 10}{10 \div 10}}} = 2 \times 1 = 2$$

$$20 \times \underset{1}{\underline{\frac{200 \div 10}{10 \div 10}}} = 20 \times 1 = 20$$

1. What happens when you divide a multiple of 10 by 10? Explain why.

_____

_____

2. What happens when you divide a multiple of 100 by 10? Explain why.

_____

_____

▶ Apply Patterns With Zeros to Division

Divide mentally.

3. $40 \div 10 =$ _____   4. $600 \div 10 =$ _____   5. $310 \div 10 =$ _____

6. $800 \div 10 =$ _____   7. $10 \div 10 =$ _____   8. $670 \div 10 =$ _____

Solve.

9. Dwight saved 100 pennies. If he splits his pennies evenly among himself and his 9 friends, how many pennies will each person get?

_____

10. The sports stadium can seat 900 people. There are 10 equal sections of seats in the stadium. How many seats are in each section?

_____

Divide by Numbers Other Than 5

Name _____   **Date** _____

▶ Discuss Puzzled Penguin Problem

The Puzzled Penguin started to solve this division problem. He knew he had a problem, so his friends suggested different ways to fix it.

$$\begin{array}{r} 7 \\ 4\overline{)3,476} \\ -\ 28 \\ \hline 6 \end{array}$$

Jacob suggested he erase the 7 and write 8 in its place. He would also need to erase the calculations and do them over. $$\begin{array}{r} 8 \\ 4\overline{)3,476} \\ -\ 32 \\ \hline 2 \end{array}$$	Fred told him to cross out the 7 and write 8 above it. He would then subtract one more 4. $$\begin{array}{r} 8 \\ \not{7} \\ 4\overline{)3,476} \\ -\ 28 \\ \hline 6 \\ -\ 4 \end{array}$$
Amad showed him that, if he used the Expanded Notation Method, he could just keep going. $$\begin{array}{r} 100 \\ 700 \\ 4\overline{)3,476} \\ -\ 2,800 \\ \hline 676 \\ -\ 400 \\ \hline 276 \end{array}$$	Kris showed him how, with the Rectangle Sections Method, he could add another section. $$\begin{array}{r} 700\ +\quad 100 \\ 4\ \begin{array}{|c|c|} \hline 3,476 & 676 \\ -\ 2,800 & -\ 400 \\ \hline \end{array} \\ \quad 676 \qquad 276 \end{array}$$

1. What was the Puzzled Penguin's problem?

_____

2. Discuss the solutions above. Which friend was right?

_____

▶ Zeros in Quotients

Solve. Discuss why a zero is needed in the quotient.

3. $6\overline{)1,842}$

4. $8\overline{)5,125}$

▶ Choose Between Calculation and Mental Math

Some problems have numbers that are easy to work with mentally. Other problems are easier to solve using pencil and paper or a calculator.

Use Mental Math

Some problems may contain numbers that are easy to work with mentally.

Example: There are 150 ribbons to be handed out at the school Field Day. There are 30 events, and the same number of ribbons will be awarded at each event. How many ribbons will be given out at each event?

The numbers in this problem are multiples of 10.
Think: $150 \div 30$ is the same as $15 \div 3$, so the anwer is 5.
Also, $30 \times 5 = 150$.

Use Calculation

If the problem asks for an exact answer and there is no noticeable pattern, then you will have to do the calculation.

Example: Last month Mandy was in school for 132 hours. She spent 6 hours in school each day. How many days did she go to school?

We need to find $132 \div 6$. This is difficult to do mentally, so use paper and pencil or a calculator: $132 \div 6 = 22$.

Solve. Then write the method you used.

1. Altogether, the members of the exercise club drink 900 bottles of water each month. Each member drinks 10 bottles. How many members are there?

2. Juan ran 270 minutes in 6 days. He ran the same number of minutes each day. How many minutes did he run each day?

Name _____   **Date** _____

▶ Check Quotients With Rounding and Estimation

Rounding and estimating can be used to check answers. Review your rounding skills, and then apply what you know to division problems.

Use rounding and estimating to decide whether each quotient makes sense.

1. $\dfrac{18\ R2}{3\overline{)56}}$

2. $\dfrac{92\ R3}{5\overline{)463}}$

3. $\dfrac{928}{6\overline{)5,568}}$

4. $\dfrac{129\ R4}{7\overline{)907}}$

Solve, using any method. Then check your answer by rounding and estimating.

5. $3\overline{)29}$

6. $6\overline{)34}$

7. $7\overline{)59}$

8. $3\overline{)72}$

9. $6\overline{)83}$

10. $7\overline{)88}$

11. $9\overline{)67}$

12. $9\overline{)95}$

13. $6\overline{)375}$

14. $2\overline{)257}$

15. $3\overline{)298}$

16. $7\overline{)384}$

17. $2\overline{)457}$

18. $3\overline{)470}$

19. $7\overline{)540}$

20. $7\overline{)628}$

21. $8\overline{)683}$

22. $9\overline{)717}$

23. $7\overline{)805}$

24. $8\overline{)869}$

25. $9\overline{)914}$

26. $6\overline{)593}$

27. $6\overline{)706}$

28. $6\overline{)969}$

29. $6\overline{)1,723}$

30. $2\overline{)2,986}$

31. $7\overline{)8,574}$

32. $6\overline{)4,652}$

33. $2\overline{)5,235}$

34. $7\overline{)7,310}$

▶ Choose Between an Estimate and an Exact Answer

Some problems require an exact answer. For others, you
only need an estimate.

Exact Answer If a problem asks for an exact answer, then you will have to do the calculation.	**Estimate** If a problem asks for a *close* answer and uses *about, approximately, almost,* or *nearly*, then you can estimate.
Example: The school cafeteria prepares 3,210 lunches each week. The same numbers of lunches are prepared 5 days each week. How many lunches are prepared each day?	**Example:** Milo has to read a 229-page book. He has 8 days to finish it. About how many pages should he read each day?
Discuss why you think this problem requires an exact answer.	Discuss why an estimate, and not an exact answer, is appropriate.

**Decide whether you need an exact answer or an estimate.
Then find the answer.**

1. Sam bought a board that was
72 inches long to make bookshelves.
He wants to cut the board into three
equal pieces and use each one for a
shelf. How long will each shelf be?

   _____

2. Sam's mother baked 62 muffins for
his class. There are 18 people in
Sam's class, including the teacher.
About how many muffins should
each person get?

   _____

3. Each 24-inch shelf can hold about
10 books. Approximately how
many inches wide is each book?

   _____

4. Malcom wants to buy 3 concert
tickets. Each ticket costs $45.50.
How much money will he need?

   _____

Estimate to Check Quotients

Class Activity

▶ Different Kinds of Remainders

Remainders in division have different meanings, depending upon the type of problem you solve.

$$\begin{array}{r} 2\ \text{R1} \\ 4\overline{)9} \\ -8 \\ \hline 1 \end{array}$$

The same numeric solution shown at the right works for the following five problems. Discuss why the remainder means something different each time.

A. The remainder is not part of the question.
Thomas has one 9-foot pine board. He needs to make 4-foot shelves for his books. How many shelves can he cut?

_____

_____

_____

B. The remainder causes the answer to be rounded up. Nine students are going on a field trip. Parents have offered to drive. If each parent can drive 4 students, how many parents need to drive?

_____

_____

_____

C. The remainder is a fractional part of the answer. One Monday Kim brought 9 apples to school. She shared them equally among herself and 3 friends. How many apples did each person get?

_____

_____

_____

_____

D. The remainder is a decimal part of the answer. Raul bought 4 toy cars for $9.00. Each car costs the same amount. How much did each car cost?

_____

_____

_____

E. The remainder is the only part needed to answer the question. Nine students have signed up to run a relay race. If each relay team can have 4 runners, how many students cannot run in the race?

_____

_____

_____

▶ Remainders As Fractions

Discuss situation C from page 293.

One Monday, Kim brought 9 apples to school. She shared them equally among herself and 3 friends. How many apples did each person get?

Kim's apples were very tasty, so every week more friends wanted to share them.

1. The next Monday, Kim brought 13 apples to share equally among herself and 5 friends. How many apples did each person get?

_____

2. The next Monday after that, Kim brought 17 apples to share equally among herself and 7 friends. How many apples did each person get?

_____

3. Write the numeric solutions to all three apple-sharing problems. Each time, write the answer first with a whole number remainder. Then on the line after the equals sign, write each answer, using a fraction. Remember that a unit fraction, $\frac{1}{d}$, means 1 of d equal parts of a whole.

$4\overline{)9}$ = _____ $6\overline{)13}$ = _____ $8\overline{)17}$ = _____

4. From week to week, did Kim get more or less apples? Why?

_____

_____

Make Sense of Remainders

Class Activity

▶ Decimal Remainders

Discuss situation D from page 293.

Raul bought 4 toy cars for $9.00. Each car cost the same amount. How much did each car cost?

5. Describe how the Digit-by-Digit solution steps show how we can write a money division problem as dollars and cents.

Step A	Step B	Step C	Step D

Step A

$$\begin{array}{r} \$2 \\ 4\overline{)\$9.00} \\ -\ 8 \\ \hline 1 \end{array}$$

Step B

$$\begin{array}{r} \$2 \\ 4\overline{)\$9.00} \\ -\ 8 \\ \hline 1.0 \end{array}$$

Step C

$$\begin{array}{r} \$2.2 \\ 4\overline{)\$9.00} \\ -\ 8 \\ \hline 1.0 \\ -\ 0.8 \\ \hline 0.2 \end{array}$$

Step D

$$\begin{array}{r} \$2.25 \\ 4\overline{)\$9.00} \\ -\ 8 \\ \hline 1.0 \\ -\ 0.8 \\ \hline 0.20 \\ -\ 0.20 \\ \hline 0 \end{array}$$

Step A: How many dollars are in the answer?

_____

How many dollars are left over?

_____

Step B: How many dimes are in the leftover dollar?

_____

Step C: How many dimes are in the answer?

_____

How many dimes are left over?

_____

Step D: How many pennies are in the leftover dimes?

_____

How many pennies are in the answer?

_____

6. Compare the numeric solutions to the apple problem and the toy-car problem. How are they different?

_____

_____

_____

7. What makes them numerically equal?

_____

8. If Raul had paid $7.00 for the cars, how much would each car have cost?

_____

Class Activity

▶ Discuss Real-World Division Problems

Solve. Then discuss the meaning of the remainder.

9. Maddie tried to divide 160 stickers equally among herself and 5 friends. There were some stickers left over, so she kept them. How many stickers did Maddie get?

_____

_____

_____

10. Kendra bought a bag of 200 cheese crackers for her class. If each student gets 7 crackers, how many students are there? How many crackers are left over?

_____

_____

_____

11. Jerry has $36.00 in his bank. He wants to give the same amount of money to each of his 8 cousins. How much money will each of Jerry's cousins get?

_____

_____

_____

12. Racheed had 87 pennies. He divided them equally among his 4 sisters. How many pennies did Racheed have after he gave his sisters their shares?

_____

_____

_____

13. Mara wants to buy some new pencil boxes for her pencil collection. She has 47 pencils. If each pencil box holds 9 pencils, how many pencil boxes does Mara need to buy?

_____

_____

_____

14. Henry's coin bank takes only nickels. Henry takes $4.42 to the bank to change for nickels. How many nickels will he get?

_____

_____

_____

15. On a separate sheet of paper, make up a problem where the remainder is a fraction. Use 36 ÷ 5.

▶ Mixed One-Step Word Problems

The fourth- and fifth-grade classes at Jackson School held a Just-for-Fun Winter Carnival. All of the students in the school were invited.

Discuss what operation you need to use to solve each problem. Then solve the problem.

1. Two students from each fourth- and fifth-grade class were on the planning committee. If Jackson School has 14 fourth- and fifth-grade classes in all, how many students planned the carnival?

_____

_____

2. To advertise the carnival, students decorated 4 hallway bulletin boards. They started with 2,025 pieces of colored paper. When they finished, they had 9 pieces left. How many pieces of paper did they use?

_____

_____

3. The parents ordered pizzas to serve at the carnival. Each pizza was cut into 8 slices. How many pizzas had to be ordered so that 1,319 people could each have one slice?

_____

_____

4. 825 students signed up to run in timed races. If exactly 6 students ran in each race, how many races were there?

_____

_____

5. At the raffle booth, 364 fourth-graders each bought one ticket to win a new school supply set. Only 8 fifth-graders each bought a ticket. How many students bought raffle tickets altogether?

_____

_____

6. Altogether, 1,263 students were enrolled in the first through fifth grades at Jackson School. On the day of the carnival, 9 students were absent. How many students could have participated in the carnival activities?

_____

_____

▶ Mixed Multistep Word Problems

Solve these problems about Pine Street School's Olympic Games.

7. At the start of the games, 193 fourth-graders were separated into three events. 87 students participated in the first event. The rest of the students were evenly divided between the other 2 events. How many students participated in the last event?

_____

_____

8. Three teams built pyramids of paper cups. Each team had exactly 176 cups to use. Team 1 used exactly half of their cups. Team 2 used 4 times as many cups as Team 3. Team 3 used 32 cups. Which team stacked the most cups?

_____

_____

9. The Parents' Club provided 357 celery sticks, 676 carrot sticks, and 488 apple slices. If each student took 3 snack pieces, how many students got a snack?

_____

_____

10. 75 first-graders and 84 second-graders skipped around the gym. After a while, only 8 students were still skipping. How many students had stopped skipping?

_____

_____

11. A team from each school had 250 foam balls and a bucket. The Jackson team dunked 6 fewer balls than the Pine Street team. The Pine Street team dunked all but 8 of their balls. How many balls did the two teams dunk in all?

_____

_____

12. When the day was over, everybody had earned at least 1 medal, and 32 students each got 2 medals. In all, 194 each of gold, silver, and bronze medals were given out. How many students played in the games?

_____

_____

Name _____   **Date** _____

▶ Calculate the Mean

The **mean** of a set of data is a number that describes the size of each of *n* equal groups made from *n* data values. You can find the mean by adding the values and dividing that sum by the number of values.

1. Davis made 4 clay pots on Friday, 7 clay pots on Saturday, and 4 clay pots on Sunday. What is the mean number of pots he made each day? Make a drawing to show how the pots for each day can be redistributed to find the mean.

_____

2. Serena, Marco, and Ray each have a fish tank. Serena has 5 fish. Marco has 6 fish. Ray has 10 fish. What is the mean number of fish that the three friends have? Make a drawing to show how they can move fish so each person has an equal share.

_____

Find the mean.

Show your work.

3. 2, 3, 5, 7, 8   Mean: _____

4. 1, 6, 13, 4, 12, 3, 10   Mean: _____

5. 29, 35, 18, 62   Mean: _____

6. 165, 917, 443, 212, 218   Mean: _____

► Word Problems With Mean

**Last week, the town of Midville hosted a county fair.
Solve these problems about the fair.**

7. The fair organizers kept track of the high temperature each day. It was 67° on Monday, 71° on Tuesday, 75° on Wednesday, 69° on Thursday, and 78° on Friday. What was the mean high temperature during the five days of the fair?

_____

_____

8. The organizers recorded the attendance each weekday. What was the mean attendance?

Day	Attendance
Monday	874
Tuesday	658
Wednesday	723
Thursday	796
Friday	909

_____

_____

9. Because the fair was so popular, the organizers decided to extend it one more day. On Saturday, 954 people attended the fair. What was the mean attendance over the 6 days?

_____

_____

10. The Johnson family attended the fair. The ticket prices for the fair are listed below.

Adults	$5.00
Teens (13–18 years old)	$4.00
Children (under 13)	$3.00

There are 2 adults and 2 teens in the Johnson family. What was the mean ticket price for the family?

_____

_____

Class Activity

▶ Word Problems With Mode and Median

The mode and median are also measures for a set of data. The mean, median, and mode are sometimes called **measures of central tendency**.

The **median** of a set of data is the middle value when the values are listed in order from least to greatest.	14, 25, 27, 32, 32 The median is 27.
If there are two middle values, the median is the mean of the two middle values (it is halfway between them).	14, 25, 32, 32 The median is the mean of 25 and 32, which is 28.5.
The **mode** of a set of data is the value that appears most often. A set of data can have one mode, several modes, or no mode (when no data value is repeated).	14, 25, 27, 32, 32 The mode is 32. 14, 25, 27, 32 There is no mode.

Solve.

Show your work.

11. There was a Guess-Your-Age booth at the fair. One afternoon, the ages of the visitors to the booth were 22, 33, 22, 30, 33, 27, and 22. Find the mean, median, and mode of the ages.

   mean: _____

   median: _____

   mode: _____

12. One more person came to the booth. His age was 67 years. Find the new mean, median, and mode of the visitors' ages.

   mean: _____

   median: _____

   mode: _____

▶ Choose the Best Measure

The mean, median, and mode are all measures of the typical value in a set of data. In some cases, one measure may be better than another to represent a set of data.

For each situation, find the mean, median, and mode of the set of data. Then decide which best represents the data.

13. Mr. Garcia's store sells cereal in 12-, 18-, and 22-ounce boxes. One week, he sold boxes that were 12-, 18-, 12-, 22-, 18-, 22-, 12-, and 12-ounce sizes.

Mean: _____

Median: _____

Mode: _____

_____

_____

_____

14. Last week, it rained for 5 days. It rained 11 mm on Monday, 8 mm on Tuesday, 22 mm on Wednesday, 9 mm on Thursday, and 10 mm on Friday.

Mean: _____

Median: _____

Mode: _____

_____

_____

_____

15. Aliya's friends spent 300, 250, 300, 750, 200, 300, 250, 350, and 900 minutes on homework.

Mean: _____

Median: _____

Mode: _____

_____

_____

_____

16. John took five math tests this term. His scores were 81, 75, 69, 81, and 54.

Mean: _____

Median: _____

Mode: _____

_____

_____

_____

17. **Math Journal** Write and solve a word problem that involves finding the mean, median, or mode of a data set.

Averages

Class Activity

Vocabulary
range

▶ Find Range

A **range** is a way to describe data, and is found by subtracting the least (or minimum) number in a set from the greatest (or maximum) number.

For example, in the set of numbers at the right, the greatest number is 28 and the least number is 15. The range of the set of numbers is 13 because 28 − 15 = 13.

greatest
↓
{16, 28, 17, 20, 15, 23}
↑
least

Find the range of each set of numbers.

18. {7, 5, 5, 1, 9, 4, 5}

range = _____

19. {68, 81, 47, 56, 19, 30}

range = _____

20. {104, 267, 199, 431}

range = _____

▶ Statistics and Bar Graphs

The data in a bar graph can be described in many ways. Some of the ways include finding the mean, median, mode (if any), and range of the data.

Use the bar graph at the right to answer the questions.

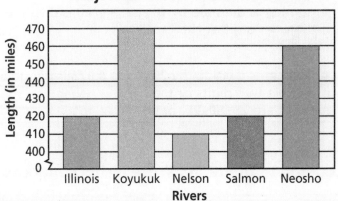

Major Rivers in North America

21. How can you tell simply by looking at the graph that the mean length is greater than 410 miles?

_____

_____

22. Explain how you can find the median simply by looking at the graph.

_____

_____

23. Which measure or measures of the data—mean, median, mode, or range—would *not* be affected if a river with a length of 450 miles was added to the graph? _____

▶ Using Divisibility Rules

When one number is **divisible** by another number, the remainder of the division of those numbers is 0. For example, 6 is divisible by 2 because 6 ÷ 2 has a quotient whose remainder is zero.

We can test greater numbers for divisibility mentally by using divisibility rules.

Summary of Rule	Example	Non-Example
A number is divisible by 2 if the ones digit of the number is 0, 2, 4, 6, or 8.	38 is divisible by 2.	73 is not divisible by 2.
A number is divisible by 5 if the ones digit of the number is 0 or 5.	295 is divisible by 5.	611 is not divisible by 5.
A number is divisible by 10 if the ones digit of the number is 0.	760 is divisible by 10.	905 is not divisible by 10.
A number is divisible by 25 if the last two digits of the number are 25, 50, 75, or 00.	4,375 is divisible by 25.	5,647 is not divisible by 25.

Complete the table. Write a check mark to show divisibility.

	30	45	75	100	165	225
1. divisible by 2						
2. divisible by 5						
3. divisible by 10						
4. divisible by 25						

5. Is every number that is divisible by 10 also divisible by 2 and by 5? Give a reason to support your answer.

_____

_____

Class Activity

▶ Multiply by 10, 100, and 1,000

Write each product. Look for a pattern.

1. $8 \times 10 =$ _____

$8 \times 100 =$ _____

$8 \times 1,000 =$ _____

4. $14 \times 10 =$ _____

$14 \times 100 =$ _____

$14 \times 1,000 =$ _____

2. $3 \times 10 =$ _____

$3 \times 100 =$ _____

$3 \times 1,000 =$ _____

5. $25 \times 10 =$ _____

$25 \times 100 =$ _____

$25 \times 1,000 =$ _____

3. $9 \times 10 =$ _____

$9 \times 100 =$ _____

$9 \times 1,000 =$ _____

6. $50 \times 10 =$ _____

$50 \times 100 =$ _____

$50 \times 1,000 =$ _____

▶ Divide by 10, 100, and 1,000

Write each quotient. Look for a pattern.

7. $360 \div 10 =$ _____

$3,600 \div 100 =$ _____

$36,000 \div 1,000 =$ _____

10. $50 \div 10 =$ _____

$500 \div 100 =$ _____

$5,000 \div 1,000 =$ _____

8. $20 \div 10 =$ _____

$200 \div 100 =$ _____

$2,000 \div 1,000 =$ _____

11. $940 \div 10 =$ _____

$9,400 \div 100 =$ _____

$94,000 \div 1,000 =$ _____

9. $730 \div 10 =$ _____

$7,300 \div 100 =$ _____

$73,000 \div 1,000 =$ _____

12. $100 \div 10 =$ _____

$1,000 \div 100 =$ _____

$10,000 \div 1,000 =$ _____

Multiply or divide.

13. $12 \times 10 =$ _____

16. $700 \div 100 =$ _____

19. $900 \times 100 =$ _____

22. $18,000 \div 1,000 =$ _____

25. $700 \times 1,000 =$ _____

14. $60 \div 10 =$ _____

17. $8 \times 1,000 =$ _____

20. $4,500 \div 100 =$ _____

23. $6 \times 100 =$ _____

26. $580 \div 10 =$ _____

15. $34 \times 100 =$ _____

18. $6,000 \div 1,000 =$ _____

21. $230 \times 10 =$ _____

24. $8,000 \div 100 =$ _____

27. $15 \times 1,000 =$ _____

Name _____ **Date** _____

Going Further

▶ Multiply by 11 and 12

Use what you know about patterns to solve the problems.

1. Mrs. Wang has 132 hats in her store. She can display 11 hats on each shelf. On how many shelves can she display hats?

$1 \times 11 =$ _____

$2 \times 11 =$ _____

$3 \times 11 =$ _____

$4 \times 11 =$ _____

$5 \times 11 =$ _____

$6 \times 11 =$ _____

$7 \times 11 =$ _____

$8 \times 11 =$ _____

$9 \times 11 =$ _____

$10 \times 11 =$ _____

$11 \times 11 =$ _____

$12 \times 11 =$ _____

2. Mr. Amos bakes dozens of rolls at his bakery. How many rolls does he need to bake if 12 customers each order a dozen rolls?

$1 \times 12 =$ _____

$2 \times 12 =$ _____

$3 \times 12 =$ _____

$4 \times 12 =$ _____

$5 \times 12 =$ _____

$6 \times 12 =$ _____

$7 \times 12 =$ _____

$8 \times 12 =$ _____

$9 \times 12 =$ _____

$10 \times 12 =$ _____

$11 \times 12 =$ _____

$12 \times 12 =$ _____

▶ Multiply and Divide by 11 and 12

Multiply or divide.

3. $120 \div 12 =$ ___
4. $11 \times 11 =$ ___
5. $99 \div 11 =$ ___
6. $11 \times 12 =$ ___

7. $132 \div 11 =$ ___
8. $96 \div 12 =$ ___
9. $77 \div 11 =$ ___
10. $144 \div 12 =$ ___

11. $8 \times 12 =$ ___
12. $108 \div 12 =$ ___
13. $84 \div 12 =$ ___
14. $121 \div 11 =$ ___

15. $110 \div 11 =$ ___
16. $72 \div 12 =$ ___
17. $66 \div 11 =$ ___
18. $12 \times 12 =$ ___

Multiply and Divide by Powers of 10

Class Activity

Name _____ **Date** _____

Vocabulary

analog
digital

▶ Tell Time on Different Clocks

An **analog** clock has a face, a shorter hour hand, and a longer minute hand.

1. Discuss how to remember which hand is which and what is the clockwise direction.

2. Write the 5s count-bys around the outside of the green clock to see minutes.

Write the time.

3.

_____

4.

_____

5.

_____

A **digital** clock shows the hour and minutes with numbers.

On a separate sheet of paper, draw an analog clock to show the time on the digital clock.

6.   AM 9:30

7.   AM 11:45

8.   PM 3:00

9. What does a digital clock usually tell us that an analog clock does not show?

_____

10. Draw digital clocks for the clocks shown in exercises 3, 4, and 5 in the space below. Give times as A.M. or P.M.

Class Activity

▶ Read Elapsed Time

You can imagine the hands moving to tell how much time has passed.

How many hours have passed since 12:00 on each clock? How many minutes?

11.

12.

13.

_____

_____

How many hours and how many minutes does the clock show? Write the time that the clock shows.

14.

15.

16.

_____ hours

_____ minutes

_____ hours

_____ minutes

_____ hours

_____ minutes

How many hours and minutes have passed between the times shown in:

17. exercises 14 and 15

18. exercises 15 and 16

19. exercises 14 and 16

_____

_____

_____

▶ Solve Problems

Show your work.

20. What operation lets you find the difference between two times numerically?

    _____

21. How many minutes will pass between 8:15 A.M. and 8:47 A.M.?

    _____

22. How many minutes will pass between 8:15 A.M. and 9:47 A.M.?

    _____

23. If you started your homework at 4:15 P.M. and finished at 5:08 P.M., how much time did you spend on your homework?

    _____

    _____

24. If you start something at 11:15 A.M. and finish at 2:30 P.M., how can you find the elapsed time?

    _____

    _____

25. You need to be at school at 8:30 A.M., and it takes you 45 minutes to get there. What time should you leave home to get there on time?

    _____

26. You practice your musical instrument for 35 minutes every day. If you start at 4:42 P.M., at what time will you finish? Why can the answer not be 4:77? What do you have to do to fix the answer?

    _____

    _____

Going Further

▶ Calculate Units of Time

Solve.

1. 12 weeks = _____ days

2. 900 seconds = _____ minutes

3. 24 hours = _____ minutes

4. 168 hours = _____ days

5. 200 years = _____ centuries

6. 25 years = _____ months

7. 720 minutes = _____ hours

8. 50 years = _____ decades

9. 20 years = _____ weeks

10. 1 day = _____ seconds

11. There are 1,000 years in a millennium. Explain how to find the number of decades in a millennium, and then name that number of decades.

_____

_____

12. Chandra jogs 3 miles every other day for exercise. Explain how to *estimate* the number of miles Chandra jogs per month. Then name that number of miles.

_____

_____

_____

13. On your next birthday, how many years old will you be? _____

Explain how to find the number of months old you will be at that time. Then find that number of months.

_____

_____

Calculator Explain how to *estimate* the number of days old you will be. Use a calculator to find that number.

_____

The Passing of Time

Class Activity

Name _____ Date _____

Vocabulary

simplify

term

▶ Properties and Algebraic Notation

We **simplify** an expression or equation by performing operations to combine like **terms**.

Use the Identity Property to simplify each expression.

1. $n + 5n =$ _____
2. $17t + t =$ _____
3. $x + 245x =$ _____

4. $9e - e =$ _____
5. $8c + c + c =$ _____
6. $(5z - z) - z =$ _____

Solve.

7. $30 \div (35 \div 7) =$ ___
8. $(72 \div 9) \div 4 =$ ___
9. $80 \div (32 \div 8) =$ ___

10. $13 - (9 - 1) =$ ___
11. $(600 - 400) - 10 =$ ___
12. $100 - (26 - 6) =$ ___

Use properties to find the value of ☐ **or** *a*.

13. $49 + 17 = \boxed{} + 49$

☐ = _____

14. $(a \cdot 2) \cdot 3 = 4 \cdot (2 \cdot 3)$

$a =$ _____

15. $\boxed{} \cdot 6 = 6 \cdot 8$

☐ = _____

16. $6 \cdot (40 + a) = (6 \cdot 40) + (6 \cdot 5)$

$a =$ ___

17. $(\boxed{} \cdot 5) + (\boxed{} \cdot 9) = 7 \cdot (5 + 9)$

☐ = ___

18. $29 + 8 = 29 + \boxed{}$ Is ☐ $= 4 + 2$ or $4 \cdot 2$? _____

19. $a \cdot 14 = 15 \cdot 14$ Is $a = 5 \cdot 3$ or $5 + 3$? _____

20. $60 + 10 = \boxed{} + 60$ Is ☐ $= 2 + 5$ or $2 \cdot 5$? _____

Class Activity

Vocabulary

evaluate

▶ Parentheses in Equations

Solve.

21. $9 \cdot n = 144$

n = _____

22. $s + 170 = 200$

s = _____

23. $105 \div h = 7$

h = _____

24. $(10 - 4) \cdot 7 = \boxed{} \cdot 7$

$\boxed{} = $ _____

25. $4 \cdot (9 - 3) = g$

g = _____

26. $(10 - 6) \div 2 = b$

b = _____

27. $9 \cdot (6 + 2) = \boxed{} \cdot 8$

$\boxed{} = $ _____

28. $\boxed{} \cdot 6 = 96$

$\boxed{} = $ _____

29. $(15 \div 3) \cdot (4 + 1) = v$

v = _____

30. $(12 - 5) - (12 \div 6) = $ _____

31. $(23 + 4) \div (8 - 5) = $ _____

32. $(24 \div 3) \cdot (12 - 7) = $ _____

33. $(22 + 8) \div (17 - 11) = $ _____

▶ Substitute a Value

To **evaluate** an expression or equation:

1) Substitute the value of each letter.
2) Then simplify the expression by performing the operations.

Evaluate each expression.

34. $a = 4$

$19 - (a + 6)$

_____

35. $a = 10$

$(80 \div a) - 5$

_____

36. $b = 3$

$(8 \div 4) \cdot (7 - b)$

_____

37. $b = 7$

$21 \div (b - 4)$

_____

38. $b = 11$

$(b + 9) \div (7 - 2)$

_____

39. $c = 8$

$(20 - 10) + (7 + c)$

_____

40. $x = 9$

$16 \cdot (13 - x)$

_____

41. $d = 3$

$(24 \div 3) \cdot (y + 7)$

_____

42. $d = 0$

$(63 \div 7) \cdot d$

_____

Vocabulary

expression

▶ Expressions

Solve.

1. Elena has purchased a phone plan that charges 10 cents for every text message she sends.

   Circle the letter of the expression below that shows the cost if Elena sends one text message each day for one week.

   a. $\$0.10 \cdot 5$ **b.** $\$0.10 \cdot 7$ **c.** $\$0.10 + 7$

2. When concert tickets are purchased online, each ticket costs $25, and for any number of tickets purchased, a service charge of $15 is added to the cost.

   Circle the letter of the expression below that represents the cost of purchasing 2 tickets.

   a. $2 \cdot (\$15 + \$25)$ **b.** $2 + \$25 \cdot \$15$ **c.** $(2 \cdot \$25) + \$15$

3. At the end of the school year, there were two more students in Trevor's class than there were at the beginning of the year.

   In each expression below, *n* represents the number of students in Trevor's class at the end of the school year. Circle the letter of the expression that represents the number of students in his class at the beginning of the year.

   a. $n - 2$ **b.** $n + 2$ **c.** $2 - n$

4. Write a real world situation to represent the expression $\$2.50 + \$1.25m$.

   _____

   _____

   _____

Class Activity

Vocabulary

inequality

▶ Inequalities

An **inequality** is a statement that two expressions are not equal.

$5 > 4$ $4 < 5$ $4 \neq 5$

5 is greater than 4   4 is less than 5   4 does not equal 5

Solve.

5. The cost of one adult admission ticket to the school musical is less than $6. Circle the letter of the expression below that represents the cost in dollars (*d*) of one adult admission ticket.

   a. $d > 6$ **b.** $d < 6$ **c.** $d = 6$

6. The odometer of a car shows that the car has traveled more than 8,000 miles. Circle the letter of the expression below that represents the distance in miles (*m*) the car has traveled.

   a. $m > 8,000$ **b.** $m < 8,000$ **c.** $m = 8,000$

7. Write a real-world situation to represent the inequality $s > 100$.

   _____

   _____

   _____

8. Write a real-world situation to represent the inequality $a \neq b$.

   _____

   _____

   _____

▶ Solve One-Step Equations

Solve each equation.

1. $m - 1 = 9$

   $m =$ _____

2. $v + 4 = 13$

   $v =$ _____

3. $c \div 5 = 10$

   $c =$ _____

4. $3 \cdot y = 18$

   $y =$ _____

5. $17 + j = 22$

   $j =$ _____

6. $6n = 48$

   $n =$ _____

7. $15 - q = 4$

   $q =$ _____

8. $36 \div p = 4$

   $p =$ _____

9. $13 + s = 26$

   $s =$ _____

▶ Choose an Equation

Choose the equation that can be used to solve each problem.

10. The cost of an item is $9.50, not including tax. The cost of the item including tax is $10.07. Which equation below can be used to find the amount of tax (t)?

    a. $\$9.50 \cdot t = \$10.07$ **b.** $t - \$9.50 = \$10.07$ **c.** $\$9.50 + t = \$10.07$

11. Cesar earns $8 for mowing a lawn. Last week he earned $32 mowing lawns. Which equation below can be used to find the number of lawns (n) he mowed last week?

    a. $\$8 \div n = \$32$ **b.** $\$32 \div \$8 = n$ **c.** $n \cdot \$32 = \$8$

12. **Challenge** Write a problem that could be solved using this equation.

    $7n = 56$

    _____

    _____

    _____

Name _____   **Date** _____

▶ Use Mental Math

Use mental math to solve each equation.

13. $2n + 1 = 9$

   $n =$ _____

14. $(c \div 2) + 3 = 4$

   $c =$ _____

15. $4h - 2 = 22$

   $h =$ _____

16. $8 \div (z + 7) = 1$

   $z =$ _____

17. $3d - 1 = 8$

   $d =$ _____

18. $(s \div 5) + 1 = 2$

   $s =$ _____

19. $9m + 4 = 31$

   $m =$ _____

20. $(p \div 3) + 2 = 9$

   $p =$ _____

21. $5j - 10 = 0$

   $j =$ _____

▶ Choose an Equation

Choose the equation that can be used to solve each problem.

22. Jacqueline earns a weekly allowance of $4. She also earns $5 for each hour she baby-sits. Last week, Jacqueline earned $29 altogether. Which equation below can be used to find the number of hours (h) that she baby-sat?

   a. $\$4 \bullet h + \$5 = \$29$ **b.** $(\$5 \bullet h) + \$4 = \$29$ **c.** $h \bullet (\$4 + \$5) = \$29$

23. Tomas bought a number of pens for 79¢ each. The tax for his purchase was 19¢, and he spent $3.35 altogether. Which equation below can be used to find the number of pens (p) Tomas bought?

   a. $79¢ + (19¢ + p) = \$3.35$ **b.** $\$3.35 = (19¢)(p) + 79¢$ **c.** $(79¢)(p) + 19¢ = \$3.35$

24. **Challenge** Write a problem that could be solved using this equation.

   $3n + 5 = 17$

   _____

   _____

   _____

One-Step and Two-Step Equations

▶ Math and Science

The butterfly and the leaf have **line symmetry.** The dashed fold line is called the **line of symmetry.**

The starfish has **rotational symmetry.** The point in the center is the **point of rotation.**

1. Why can we say that the butterfly and the leaf have line symmetry?

   _____

   _____

2. Why can we say that the starfish has rotational symmetry?

   _____

   _____

3. On a separate piece of paper, draw a picture of something in nature that has line symmetry. Include a line of symmetry.

4. On a separate piece of paper, draw a picture of something in nature that has rotational symmetry. Show the point of rotation.

Class Activity

▶ Which Would You Prefer...?

1. You can choose either amount of money. Which amount would you prefer to have? Explain your choice.

_____

_____

2. You will receive free passes for rides at a park. Would you prefer 107 free passes or 170 free passes? Explain, using words and pictures.

_____

_____

3. You want to set the thermostat at a comfortable room temperature. You have the choice of the two temperatures shown. Which temperature would you prefer? Explain your choice.

_____

_____

4. You are designing a 24-square-foot garden with a brick border. It can measure 3 feet by 8 feet or 4 feet by 6 feet. You want to save money on bricks. Which would you prefer? Explain your choice.

_____

_____

Use Mathematical Processes

Solve.

1. $8\overline{)25}$ 2. $7\overline{)56}$ 3. $6\overline{)216}$ 4. $4\overline{)306}$

5. $3\overline{)927}$ 6. $2\overline{)5,309}$ 7. 234×100 8. $750 \div 10$

Evaluate each expression.

9. $m = 3$
   $19 - (2 \times m)$ _____

10. $b = 6$
    $(36 \div 9) \cdot (b + 3)$ _____

11. $t = 4$
    $14 \cdot (5 - t)$ _____

Solve each equation.

12. $n \cdot 6 = 24$
    $n =$ _____

13. $43 - c = 36$
    $c =$ _____

14. $8 \cdot (11 - v) = 56$
    $v =$ _____

Use rounding and estimation to decide whether each answer makes sense. Explain your work.

15. $\overset{49 \text{ R}3}{6\overline{)297}}$ _____

16. $\overset{36}{7\overline{)182}}$ _____

Solve.   *Show your work.*

17. A club is renting vans for a trip. Six students will ride in each van. The remaining students will ride in other cars. If 28 students are going on the trip, how many students will ride in other cars?

    _____

18. Mr. Walsh cuts a 31-foot-long board into 5 pieces. How long is each piece?

    _____

Solve.

Show your work.

19. Tara worked for 4 hours and earned $15.00. How much did she earn each hour?

_____

20. How many packages of 8 buns would Mr. Johnson need for 233 hamburgers?

_____

21. Conchetta leaves her house at 3:00 P.M. to attend a concert. The concert starts at 3:15 P.M. and lasts for 2 hours 30 minutes. At what time does the concert end?

_____

22. Mrs. Suarez wants to give 3 crackers to each of her 27 students. If there are 6 crackers in a package, how many packages will she need?

_____

_____

23. Jan had 245 apples. She used 175 of them to make applesauce. She plans to use the rest to make 10 apple pies. How many apples will be used in each pie?

_____

Use this information for problems 24 and 25.

On her first four tests, Clara scored 80, 83, 79, and 86.

24. What was her mean test score?

_____

25. **Extended Response** If she scores 87 on her final test, will Clara's mean score go up or down? Explain.

_____

_____

Name _____ **Date** _____

Class Activity

▶ Identify Patterns

A **pattern** is a sequence that can be described by a rule.
A **sequence** is a set of objects, shapes, or numbers
arranged in a specific order.

Study each repeating pattern. Then answer the questions.

1.

   a. Describe the pattern and its repeating unit, using words.

   _____

   _____

   b. Draw the next shape in the pattern.

2.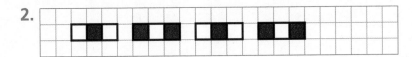

   a. Which sequence of letters below best represents the pattern?

     A B C A B C   A B A B   A B C D A B C D

   b. Draw the next shape in the pattern.

3.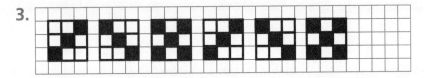

   a. Write a sequence of letters to represent the pattern. _____

   b. Draw the next shape in the pattern.

▶ Extend Patterns

4.

   a. Draw a shape to extend the pattern.

   b. Draw a **different** shape to extend the pattern.

► Extend Growing Patterns

A **term** of a pattern is a number, shape, or object in that pattern.

Study each growing pattern. Then answer the questions.

5.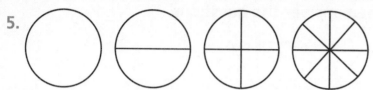

    ___   ___   ___   ___

   a. Under each term in the pattern, write the number of equal parts.

   b. How many equal parts are in the fifth term of the pattern? _____

   c. Write a rule for finding the number of equal parts in the fifth term.

_____

_____

6.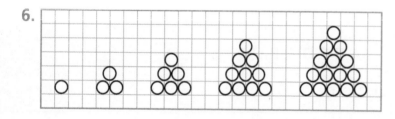

   ___   ___   ___   ___

   a. Under each term in the pattern, write the number of circles.

   b. How many circles will be in the sixth term of the pattern? _____

   c. Describe the pattern, using words.

_____

_____

_____

► **Act It Out**

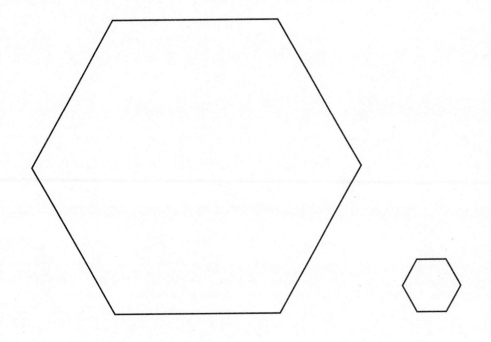

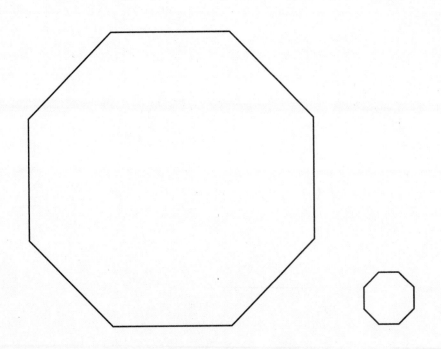

Dear Family,

In our math class, we are learning about patterns, functions, and graphs. The kinds of patterns we are studying include numerical patterns and geometric patterns. An example of each is shown below.

Numerical Pattern

800, 400, 200, 100, 50, …

Geometric Pattern

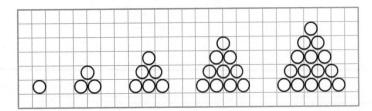

We are also studying functions and graphs. A function, shown in the table below, is a relationship shared by two sets of numbers. We are also learning to graph functions. The graph of a function, also shown below, gives us a different way of seeing the relationship that is shared by the two sets of numbers.

x	y
0	2
2	4
4	6
6	8
8	10

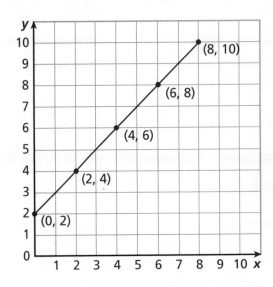

If you have any questions or comments, please call or write to me.

Sincerely,
Your child's teacher

Estimada familia:

En nuestra clase de matemáticas, estamos aprendiendo sobre patrones funciones y gráficas. Entre los patrones que estamos estudiando se encuentran los patrones numéricos y los patrones geométricos. A continuación mostramos un ejemplo de cada uno.

Patrón numérico

800, 400, 200, 100, 50, ...

Patrón geométrico

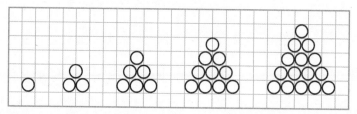

También estamos estudiando funciones y gráficas. Una función, como la que aparece en la tabla de abajo, es una relación entre dos conjuntos de números. En la clase también estamos aprendiendo a graficar funciones. La gráfica de una función, que asimismo aparece debajo, muestra de una manera diferente la relación que existe entre los dos conjuntos de números.

x	y
0	2
2	4
4	6
6	8
8	10

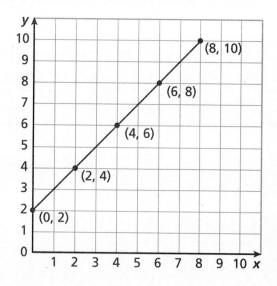

Si tiene alguna pregunta o comentario, por favor comuníquese conmigo.

Atentamente,
El maestro de su niño

Geometric Patterns

▶ Extending Sequences in More Than One Way

1. The first three terms of a pattern are shown below.

1 2 4

What could the next three terms be? Explain how you know.

_____

_____

_____

2. Look again at the pattern and your answer in exercise 1. Extend the pattern a different way.

_____

_____

_____

▶ Growing Patterns

The patterns below involve one operation. Describe each pattern, and identify the next term in it.

3. 775, 800, 825, 850, 875, ... _____

4. 3, 6, 12, 24, 48, ... _____

5. At a camera store, one color photo enlargement costs $2.50, two cost $4.50, three cost $6.50, and four cost $8.50. If the costs follow a pattern, what is likely to be the cost of eight enlargements?

_____

6. Caitlyn lives in the tenth house on Elm Street. The first house on Elm Street is numbered 1. The second is 5. The third is 9. The fourth is 13. If this pattern continues, what is Amy's house number likely to be?

_____

▶ Shrinking Patterns

The patterns below involve one operation. Describe each pattern, and identify the next term in it.

7. 800, 400, 200, 100, 50, … _____

8. 72, 63, 54, 45, 36, … _____

9. 132, 119, 106, 93, 80, … _____

10. 100,000 10,000 1,000 100 10 … _____

11. Write your own growing or shrinking pattern. Challenge a classmate to identify the repeating terms in your pattern, name the next few terms in the pattern, and if possible, extend the pattern two different ways.

_____

_____

▶ Patterns With Two Operations

The patterns below involve two operations. Describe each pattern, and identify the next two terms in it.

12. 1, 3, 4, 12, 13, 39, 40, 120, 121, … _____

13. 2, 6, 5, 15, 14, 42, 41, 123, … _____

14. The math club's problem of the week is to name the next two terms in the pattern that is shown below.

$$8, \ 5, \ 10, \ 7, \ 14, \ 11, \ 22, \ …$$

Describe the pattern, and name the next two terms.

_____

_____

▶ Input/Output Machines

Use the input/output machines to complete
the tables.

1.

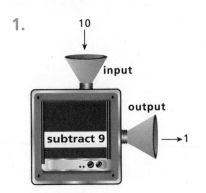

Input	Output
10	1
13	
16	
22	
25	

2.

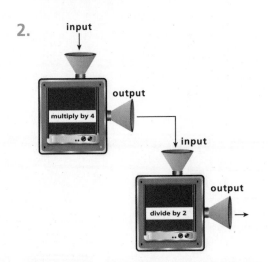

Input	Output
1	
7	
20	
4	
11	

▶ Using Inverse Operations

Use the given operation, or its
inverse operation, to find the missing values in each table.

3.

Add 3					
Input	1	4			9
Output			8	15	

4.

Divide by 10					
Input	20		10	50	
Output		6			10

Class Activity

Name _____

Date _____

Vocabulary

function
rule

▶ One-Operation Functions

A table is a way to display a function. A **function** is a mathematical relationship that is shared by two sets of numbers. A **rule** describes the relationship.

For each function below, one operation is given. Use the operation to complete the table.

5.

Subtract 1					
Input	4	2		5	
Output			8		0

6.

Add 5					
Input	2		3		7
Output		10		6	

7.

Multiply by 11					
Input		12		9	
Output	77		110		121

▶ Two-Operation Functions

For each function below, two operations are given. Use the operations to complete the table.

8.

Multiply by 3, then subtract 1					
Input	1	2	6	4	7
Output					

9.

Divide by 2, then add 3					
Input	4	2	10	8	6
Output					

Functions

▶ Write a Rule

This table shows that the number of legs is a function of the number of dogs. Use the table to complete exercise 11.

Number of dogs	1	2	3	4	5	6	7	8
Number of legs	4	8	12	16	20	24	28	32

10. Using words, write the rule of the function.

_____

_____

▶ Make a Table

11. Write a function rule in words that includes two operations.

_____

_____

12. Write your answer for exercise 12 in the first row of the table below. In the second row of the table, write five inputs. Then use the rule and write the missing outputs.

Rule: _____				
Input				
Output				

13. At a bakery, bran muffins are baked by the dozen. In the table below, write a rule to describe the relationship. Then complete the table to show the number of muffins baked for any number of dozen.

Rule: _____						

Name _____   **Date** _____

▶ Functions and Equations

The function below describes the number of legs (*l*) for any number of spiders (*s*).

Number of spiders (*s*)	1	2	3	4	5	6	7	8
Number of legs (*l*)	8	16	24	32	40	48	56	64

14. Using the variables *s* and *l*, write an equation which shows that the number of legs (*l*) is a function of the number of spiders (*s*). _____

15. Write an equation that uses the variables *x* and *y* and shows *y* as a function of *x*.

x	0	1	2	3	4
y	1	2	3	4	5

_____

Solve.

16. Each ticket to a school musical costs $6. Write an equation to represent the cost in dollars (*d*) for any number of tickets (*t*). _____

   Jon spent $30 buying tickets. Explain how to find the number of tickets he bought. Then name the number of tickets.

   _____

17. **Challenge** Copy the table below. Write an algebraic rule that contains parentheses and three operations— multiplication, addition, and subtraction. Then write input and output values to complete the table.

Rule: _____				
Input				
Output				

Vocabulary

coordinate plane
ordered pair
origin

▶ Read Points

Use the **coordinate plane** to answer the questions.

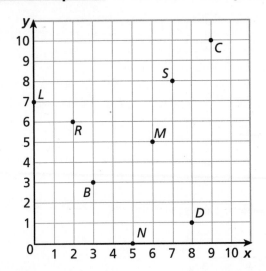

1. An **ordered pair** is used to describe the location of any point in the coordinate plane. An ordered pair consists of two coordinates.

   a. The first coordinate represents distance along which axis? _____

   b. The second coordinate represents distance along which axis? _____

2. The **origin** of the coordinate plane is the point at (0, 0). Why is the origin an important point?

   _____

   _____

Write an ordered pair to represent the location of each point.

3. point *B* _____   4. point *C* _____   5. point *D* _____   6. point *L* _____

7. point *M* _____   8. point *N* _____   9. point *R* _____   10. point *S* _____

11. Do (1, 4) and (4, 1) represent the same point? Explain.

   _____

   _____

Class Activity

▶ Plot Points

Use the coordinate plane below to complete exercises 12–26.

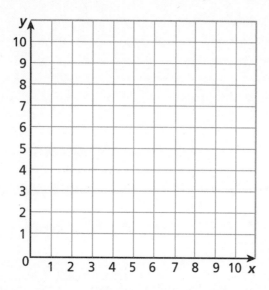

Plot and label a point at each location.

12. point *J* at (5, 4)

13. point *Q* at (1, 9)

14. point *Y* at (2, 0)

15. point *W* at (0, 4)

16. point *K* at (4, 5)

17. point *R* at (8, 3)

18. point *B* at (6, 1)

19. point *V* at (3, 8)

20. point *L* at (10, 0)

21. point *P* at (7, 10)

22. point *C* at (0, 6)

23. point *Z* at (9, 7)

Use the coordinate plane above to complete the following exercises. You may use a ruler and draw line segments if you find it helpful.

24. Name three points that form an acute angle. _____

25. Name three points that form an obtuse angle. _____

26. Name three points that form a right angle. _____

The Coordinate Plane

▶ Horizontal and Vertical Distance

27. Plot a point at (1, 10). Label the point *A*.
    Plot a point at (1, 7). Label the point *B*.
    Plot a point at (8, 10). Label the point *C*.
    Plot a point at (8, 7). Label the point *D*.
    Connect the points to form a quadrilateral.

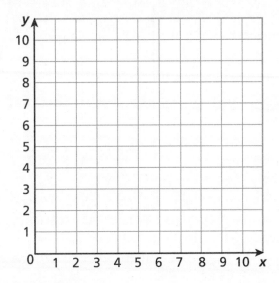

28. Explain how subtraction can be used to find the
    lengths of line segments *AB* and *AC*.

    _____

    _____

    _____

29. In the coordinate plane above, draw a rectangle that is
    not a square.

30. What ordered pairs represent the vertices of the
    rectangle?

    _____

31. Write a subtraction number sentence to represent
    the length of the rectangle, and write a subtraction
    number sentence to represent its width.

    _____

Going Further

▶ Draw Translations

1. Draw a **translation** of square *ABCD* five units down.

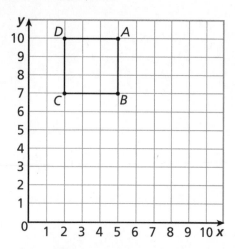

Write the coordinates of the vertices of the translated square.

_____

2. Draw a translation of triangle *XYZ* six units to the left.

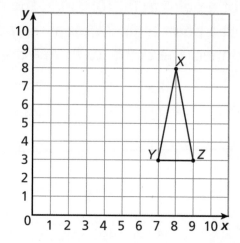

Write the coordinates of the vertices of the translated triangle.

_____

▶ Draw Reflections

3. Draw a **reflection** of triangle *PQR* across the vertical line.

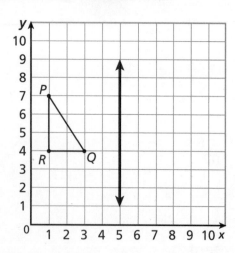

Write the coordinates of the vertices of the reflected triangle.

_____

4. Draw a reflection of parallelogram *KLMN* across the horizontal line.

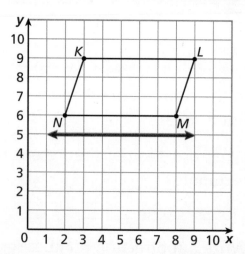

Write the coordinates of the vertices of the translated parallelogram.

_____

Class Activity

▶ Graph Points From a Table

1. The *x*- and *y*-values in the table represent a function. Write a rule that describes how to find *y*.

   _____

x	y
0	2
2	4
4	6
6	8
8	10

2. The values in each row of the table represent an ordered pair. Write the ordered pairs.

   _____

3. Each ordered pair represents a point. Plot and label each point. Then use a ruler to connect the points.

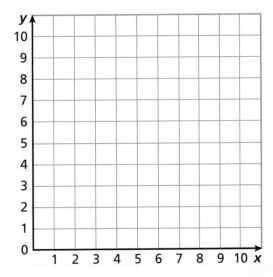

4. Compare the *y*-coordinate of each point to its *x*-coordinate. Describe the relationship, using words.

   _____

   _____

5. How does the pattern of points in the graph compare to the pattern of numbers in the table?

   _____

Name _____   **Date** _____

Class Activity

▶ Graph an Equation

6. Complete the table at the right to show how to find the number of feet (*f*) for a number of yards (*y*).

7. Write an equation to represent the relationship.

_____

8. Graph the relationship.

1 yard = 3 feet	
y	*f*
1	3
2	
3	
4	

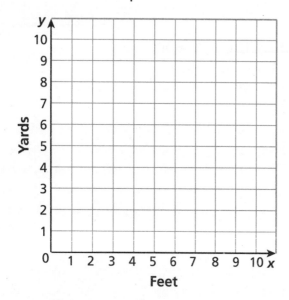

9. Complete the table below to show the relationship of the Perimeter (*P*) of an equilateral triangle to the length of one of its sides (*s*). Then graph the relationship.

P = 3s	
P	*s*
	1
	2
	3
	4

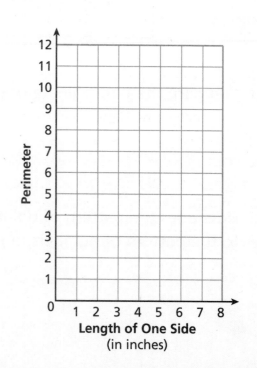

Length of One Side
(in inches)

Graph a Function

▶ Predict Points On a Line

A dripping faucet leaked 25 mL of water in 10 minutes.

10. Complete the table below to show the amount of water that will leak in 0 minutes, 10 minutes, 20 minutes, and 30 minutes.

Time (min)	0	10	20	30
Amount of Water (mL)				

11. Graph the points in the table and draw a ray to connect them. Then extend the ray as far as possible.

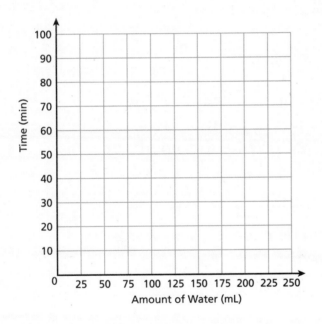

12. About how long will it take to collect 150 mL of water? _____

13. About how long will it take to collect 250 mL of water? _____

14. About how long will it take to collect 1 liter of water? (1 liter = 1,000 milliliters) Explain how you know.

_____

_____

Name _____ **Date** _____

▶ Draw Paths

1. On the grid, plot a point at (1, 10) and label the point *A*, plot a point at (1, 7) and label the point *B*.

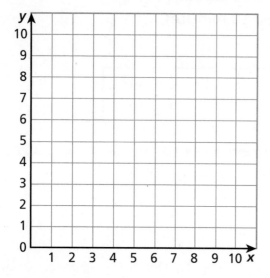

2. Using only horizontal and vertical grid lines, identify four different paths from point *A* to point *B*. Use a different color to draw each path. Write the lengths of the paths on the line below.

_____

3. Choose one of your paths and describe it, using words such as *left, right, up,* or *down*.

_____

_____

4. **Challenge** The coordinate plane at the top of the page measures 10 units by 10 units. Is it possible to draw a path that begins at one point, ends at the same point, and is more than 100 units long if you cannot retrace any part of your path or cross it at any time? On a separate sheet of paper, explain your answer.

Graph a Function

Vocabulary

continuous data

► Analyze Data

The tables show continuous data. Use the tables to answer the questions.

1. Is the trend of the cottonwood-tree data increasing or decreasing? Give a reason to support your answer.

   _____

   _____

   _____

   _____

Growth of a Cottonwood Tree	
Age (in years)	Height (in feet)
0	0
1	12
2	17
3	22

2. How would you describe the average speed of the bicycle for the first three hours of the trip?

   _____

   _____

   _____

A Bicycle Trip	
Time (in hours)	Average Speed (in miles per hour)
0	0
1	16
2	10
3	12

3. Suppose you were asked to predict what the fifth row of data would be like for one table on this page. Which table would you choose to make a prediction for? Explain why.

   _____

   _____

   _____

   _____

   _____

A Driving Trip	
Time (in hours)	Distance (in miles)
0	0
1	60
2	120
3	120

Class Activity

▶ Compare Tables and Graphs

4. Compare the data in the table below to the graph of the data.

Growth of a Cottonwood Tree	
Age (in years)	**Height (in feet)**
0	0
1	12
2	17
3	22

Does the graph correctly represent the data in the table? Explain why or why not.

_____

_____

_____

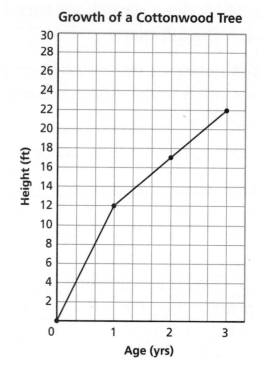

Growth of a Cottonwood Tree

5. Compare the data in the table below to the graph of the data.

A Driving Trip	
Time (in hours)	**Distance (in miles)**
0	0
1	60
2	120
3	120

Does the graph correctly represent the data in the table? Explain why or why not.

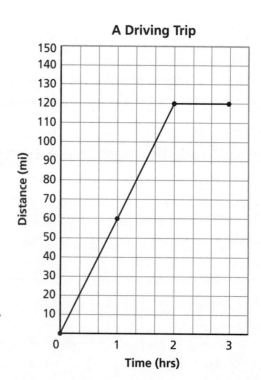

A Driving Trip

Line Graphs

▶ Analyze Line Graphs

Use the graphs to answer the questions.

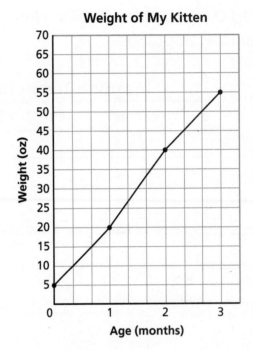

Weight of My Kitten

6. What was the weight of the kitten at birth and at each month?

_____

_____

7. What is a reasonable estimate of the weight of the kitten at the age of 4 months? Give a reason to support your answer.

_____

_____

_____

8. This graph shows the different speeds at which a bicyclist is traveling. Which portion of the graph shows the bicyclist coasting down a steep hill? Explain your answer.

_____

_____

_____

_____

_____

_____

_____

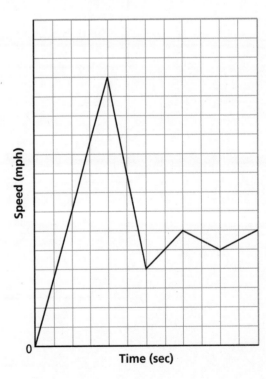

Name _____ **Date** _____

► Make a Line Graph

9. On the grid below, make a line graph that displays the data in the table.

Morning Temperatures	
Time	Temperature (°F)
3 A.M.	3
6 A.M.	0
9 A.M.	6
12 P.M.	15

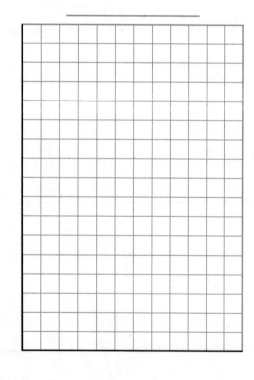

Line Graphs

Name _____   **Date** _____

1. Draw the next shape in the pattern.

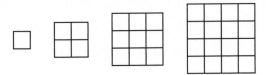

2. The pattern below involves two operations. Write a rule for the pattern, and then identify the next term in it.

   5, 9, 17, 33, 65, 129, … _____

3. Write the rule, and use it to complete the function table.

Rule:								
Input	3		8		1	9	4	11
Output	33	110		132	11		44	

Use the line graph for exercises 4–6.

4. Which one-hour period of time showed the greatest temperature change?

   _____

5. Was the temperature change in exercise 4 an increase or a decrease?

   _____

6. What is a reasonable estimate of the 7 P.M. temperature? Give a reason to support your answer.

   _____

   _____

   _____

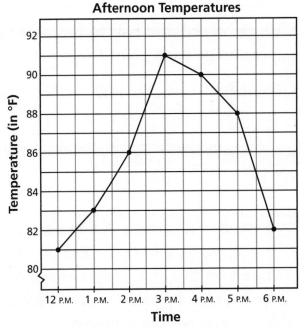

7. **a.** Each ticket to a pep rally costs $2. Write an equation to represent the cost in dollars (*d*) for any number of tickets (*t*).

b. A family spent $10 buying tickets. Explain how to find the number of tickets that were purchased, and then write the number of tickets.

Use the coordinate plane for exercises 8 and 9.

8. Each ordered pair in the table below represents a point. Plot a point in the coordinate plane at each location.

x	y
1	4
7	2
0	9
8	10
4	0

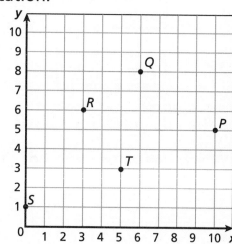

9. Write an ordered pair to represent the location of each point.

a. Point *P*   **b.** Point *Q*   **c.** Point *R*

d. Point *S*   **e.** Point *T*

10. **Extended Response** A line passes through the points (1, 3), (3, 5), and (5, 7). Explain how to find another point on the line. Then write the coordinates of that point. Make a table or use the coordinate plane above to help solve the problem.

Name _____   **Date** _____

Class Activity

Vocabulary

fraction
denominator
numerator
unit fraction

▶ Understand Unit Fractions

A **fraction** is a quantity made from equal parts of a whole.

| 1 whole | → | | → | | $\frac{5}{12}$ |

fracture 1 whole
into 12 equal parts   take 5 parts

$$\frac{n}{d} \qquad \frac{\text{numerator}}{\text{denominator}} \qquad \frac{\underline{\text{number of equal parts in this fraction}}}{\text{total equal } \underline{\text{divided}} \text{ parts in the whole}}$$

A **unit fraction** is a fraction whose numerator is 1. It shows one $\frac{1}{d}$ of d equal parts of a whole.

Fold your fraction strips to show each chain of unit fractions. Then name and write the fraction that each chain represents.

1. $\frac{1}{3} + \frac{1}{3} =$ _____

2. $\frac{1}{8} + \frac{1}{8} + \frac{1}{8} + \frac{1}{8} + \frac{1}{8} =$ _____

3. $\frac{1}{6} + \frac{1}{6} + \frac{1}{6} + \frac{1}{6} =$ _____

4. $\frac{1}{12} + \frac{1}{12} + \frac{1}{12} + \frac{1}{12} + \frac{1}{12} + \frac{1}{12} =$ _____

5. $\frac{1}{4} + \frac{1}{4} =$ _____

6. $\frac{1}{12} + \frac{1}{12} + \frac{1}{12} + \frac{1}{12} + \frac{1}{12} + \frac{1}{12} + \frac{1}{12} + \frac{1}{12} =$ _____

7. $\frac{1}{8} + \frac{1}{8} + \frac{1}{8} + \frac{1}{8} + \frac{1}{8} + \frac{1}{8} + \frac{1}{8} =$ _____

Write the word name of each fraction.

8. $\frac{3}{4}$ 9. $\frac{1}{3}$ 10. $\frac{11}{12}$ 11. $\frac{7}{8}$

_____   _____   _____   _____

Class Activity

▶ Patterns in Fraction Strips

12. Describe patterns and relationships you see in these fraction strips.

_____

_____

1	1

| $\frac{1}{2}$ | $\frac{1}{2}$ | $\frac{2}{2}$ |

| $\frac{1}{3}$ | $\frac{1}{3}$ | $\frac{1}{3}$ | $\frac{3}{3}$ |

| $\frac{1}{4}$ | $\frac{1}{4}$ | $\frac{1}{4}$ | $\frac{1}{4}$ | $\frac{4}{4}$ |

| $\frac{1}{5}$ | $\frac{1}{5}$ | $\frac{1}{5}$ | $\frac{1}{5}$ | $\frac{1}{5}$ | $\frac{5}{5}$ |

| $\frac{1}{6}$ | $\frac{1}{6}$ | $\frac{1}{6}$ | $\frac{1}{6}$ | $\frac{1}{6}$ | $\frac{1}{6}$ | $\frac{6}{6}$ |

| $\frac{1}{7}$ | $\frac{1}{7}$ | $\frac{1}{7}$ | $\frac{1}{7}$ | $\frac{1}{7}$ | $\frac{1}{7}$ | $\frac{1}{7}$ | $\frac{7}{7}$ |

| $\frac{1}{8}$ | $\frac{1}{8}$ | $\frac{1}{8}$ | $\frac{1}{8}$ | $\frac{1}{8}$ | $\frac{1}{8}$ | $\frac{1}{8}$ | $\frac{1}{8}$ | $\frac{8}{8}$ |

| $\frac{1}{9}$ | $\frac{1}{9}$ | $\frac{1}{9}$ | $\frac{1}{9}$ | $\frac{1}{9}$ | $\frac{1}{9}$ | $\frac{1}{9}$ | $\frac{1}{9}$ | $\frac{1}{9}$ | $\frac{9}{9}$ |

| $\frac{1}{10}$ | $\frac{1}{10}$ | $\frac{1}{10}$ | $\frac{1}{10}$ | $\frac{1}{10}$ | $\frac{1}{10}$ | $\frac{1}{10}$ | $\frac{1}{10}$ | $\frac{1}{10}$ | $\frac{1}{10}$ | $\frac{10}{10}$ |

▶ Chains of Unit Fractions

Fold your fraction strips to show each fraction. Then say and write the chain of unit fractions that describes each fraction.

13. $\frac{3}{4} =$ _____

14. $\frac{3}{8} =$ _____

15. $\frac{8}{8} =$ _____

16. $\frac{2}{12} =$ _____

17. $\frac{3}{12} =$ _____

18. $\frac{3}{6} =$ _____

19. $\frac{5}{12} =$ _____

20. $\frac{2}{3} =$ _____

21. $\frac{6}{8} =$ _____

22. $\frac{5}{6} =$ _____

▶ Fractions as Parts of a Whole

Jon made a large sandwich for the 6 people in his family. He asked his father to help him cut it into 6 equal pieces. To do this, they made a paper cutting guide as long as the sandwich. Jon folded the paper into 6 equal lengths, and his father used it to cut the sandwich into equal pieces.

Solve.

23. If each person ate 1 piece of the sandwich, what fraction of the sandwich did each person eat? Fold your 6-part fraction strip to show the fraction of the whole sandwich that each person ate.

_____

24. How many pieces of the whole sandwich did Jon's mother and father eat together? Fold your fraction strip to show the fraction of the whole sandwich Jon's mother and father ate in all. _____

25. After Jon's mother and father got their pieces, what fraction of the sandwich was left?

_____

26. If Jon and each of his sisters shared the remaining sandwich equally, how many sisters does Jon have?

_____

27. What ideas about fractions did we use to answer the questions about Jon's sandwich?

_____

28. **On the Back** Write a word problem in which you might need to divide a whole into equal parts.

Understand Fractions

Dear Family,

Your child has experience with fractions through comparisons, measurements, and remainders in division. Unit 9 of *Math Expressions* builds on this experience. The main goals of this unit are to:

- understand the meaning of fractions
- compare fractions with like and unlike denominators
- add and subtract fractions and mixed numbers with like and unlike denominators
- multiply a fraction by a whole number and a whole number by a fraction

Your child will use fraction bars and fraction strips to gain a visual and conceptual understanding of fractions as parts of a whole. Later, your child will use these models to add and subtract fractions, convert between improper fractions and mixed numbers, and find equivalent fractions. Your child will also learn how to use a multiplication table to find equivalent fractions.

Examples of Fraction Bar Modeling:

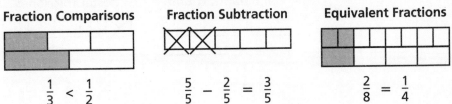

Fraction Comparisons	Fraction Subtraction	Equivalent Fractions
$\frac{1}{3} < \frac{1}{2}$	$\frac{5}{5} - \frac{2}{5} = \frac{3}{5}$	$\frac{2}{8} = \frac{1}{4}$

In later lessons of this unit, your child will be introduced to the number-line model for fractions. Students name fractions corresponding to given lengths on the number line and identify lengths corresponding to given fractions. They also see that there are many equivalent fraction names for any given length.

Your child will apply this knowledge about fractions and fraction operations to solve mixed word problems, including problems involving probability and comparisons.

If you have questions or problems, please contact me.

Sincerely,
Your child's teacher

Estimada familia:

Su niño ha usado fracciones al hacer comparaciones, mediciones y en los residuos de la división. La Unidad 9 de *Math Expressions* amplía esta experiencia. Los objetivos principales de la unidad son:

- comprender el significado de las fracciones

- comparar fracciones con denominadores iguales y distintos

- sumar y restar fracciones y números mixtos con denominadores iguales y distintos

- multiplicar una fracción por un número entero y un número entero por una fracción

Su niño usará barras y tiras de fracciones para comprender y visualizar el concepto de las fracciones como partes de un entero. Luego, usará estos modelos para sumar y restar fracciones, convertir fracciones impropias y números mixtos, y hallar fracciones equivalentes. También aprenderá a usar una tabla de multiplicación para hallar fracciones equivalentes.

Ejemplos de modelos con barras de fracciones:

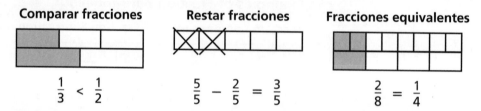

Comparar fracciones

$$\frac{1}{3} < \frac{1}{2}$$

Restar fracciones

$$\frac{5}{5} - \frac{2}{5} = \frac{3}{5}$$

Fracciones equivalentes

$$\frac{2}{8} = \frac{1}{4}$$

Más adelante en esta unidad, su niño verá el modelo de la recta numérica para las fracciones. Los estudiantes nombrarán las fracciones que correspondan a determinadas longitudes en la recta numérica e identificarán longitudes que corresponden a fracciones dadas. También observarán que hay muchos nombres de fracciones equivalentes para una longitud determinada.

Su niño aplicará este conocimiento de las fracciones y operaciones con fracciones para resolver problemas verbales variados, que incluyen problemas de probabilidad y comparaciones.

Si tiene alguna duda o comentario, por favor comuníquese conmigo.

Atentamente,
El maestro de su niño

Understand Fractions

► Fifths That Add to 1

Every afternoon, student volunteers help the school librarian put returned books back on the shelves. The librarian puts the books in equal piles on a cart.

One day Jean and Maria found 5 equal piles on the return cart. They knew there were different ways they could share the job of reshelving the books. They drew fraction bars to help them find all the possibilities.

1. On each fifths bar, circle two groups of fifths to show one way the girls could share the work. (Each bar should show a different possibility.) Then complete the equation next to each bar to show their shares.

1 whole = all of the books				
$\frac{1}{5}$	$\frac{1}{5}$	$\frac{1}{5}$	$\frac{1}{5}$	$\frac{1}{5}$
$\frac{1}{5}$	$\frac{1}{5}$	$\frac{1}{5}$	$\frac{1}{5}$	$\frac{1}{5}$
$\frac{1}{5}$	$\frac{1}{5}$	$\frac{1}{5}$	$\frac{1}{5}$	$\frac{1}{5}$
$\frac{1}{5}$	$\frac{1}{5}$	$\frac{1}{5}$	$\frac{1}{5}$	$\frac{1}{5}$

1 whole   Jean's share   Maria's share

$$\frac{5}{5} = \frac{}{5} + \frac{}{5}$$

$$\frac{5}{5} = \frac{}{5} + \frac{}{5}$$

$$\frac{5}{5} = \frac{}{5} + \frac{}{5}$$

$$\frac{5}{5} = \frac{}{5} + \frac{}{5}$$

▶ Sixths That Add to 1

The librarian put 6 equal piles of returned books on the cart for Liu and Henry to reshelf. They also drew fraction bars.

2. On each sixths bar, circle two groups of sixths to show one way that Liu and Henry could share the work. (Each bar should show a different possibility.) Then complete the equation next to each bar to show their shares.

1 whole = all of the books					
$\frac{1}{6}$	$\frac{1}{6}$	$\frac{1}{6}$	$\frac{1}{6}$	$\frac{1}{6}$	$\frac{1}{6}$
$\frac{1}{6}$	$\frac{1}{6}$	$\frac{1}{6}$	$\frac{1}{6}$	$\frac{1}{6}$	$\frac{1}{6}$
$\frac{1}{6}$	$\frac{1}{6}$	$\frac{1}{6}$	$\frac{1}{6}$	$\frac{1}{6}$	$\frac{1}{6}$
$\frac{1}{6}$	$\frac{1}{6}$	$\frac{1}{6}$	$\frac{1}{6}$	$\frac{1}{6}$	$\frac{1}{6}$
$\frac{1}{6}$	$\frac{1}{6}$	$\frac{1}{6}$	$\frac{1}{6}$	$\frac{1}{6}$	$\frac{1}{6}$

1 whole   Liu's share   Henry's share

$\frac{6}{6} = \frac{}{6} + \frac{}{6}$

$\frac{6}{6} = \frac{}{6} + \frac{}{6}$

$\frac{6}{6} = \frac{}{6} + \frac{}{6}$

$\frac{6}{6} = \frac{}{6} + \frac{}{6}$

$\frac{6}{6} = \frac{}{6} + \frac{}{6}$

▶ Find the Unknown Partner

Write the fraction that will complete each equation.

3. $1 = \frac{7}{7} = \frac{1}{7} + $ _____

4. $1 = \frac{4}{4} = \frac{3}{4} + $ _____

5. $1 = \frac{8}{8} = \frac{3}{8} + $ _____

6. $1 = \frac{5}{5} = \frac{2}{5} + $ _____

7. $1 = \frac{3}{3} = \frac{2}{3} + $ _____

8. $1 = \frac{10}{10} = \frac{6}{10} + $ _____

9. $1 = \frac{6}{6} = \frac{2}{6} + $ _____

10. $1 = \frac{8}{8} = \frac{5}{8} + $ _____

11. $\frac{3}{7} + r = \frac{5}{7}$ $r = $ _____

12. $y + \frac{2}{5} = \frac{3}{5}$ $y = $ _____

13. $m + \frac{1}{3} = \frac{2}{3}$ $m = $ _____

14. $\frac{1}{6} + c = \frac{5}{6}$ $c = $ _____

Fraction Partners of One Whole

▶ Discuss and Compare Fractions

1. Puzzled Penguin is trying to understand fractions. Discuss the patterns you see in the fraction bars he made.

| 1 | | | | | | | | | | | | $\frac{1}{1}$ |

| $\frac{1}{2}$ | | | | | | $\frac{1}{2}$ | | | | | | $\frac{2}{2}$ |

| $\frac{1}{3}$ | | | | $\frac{1}{3}$ | | | | $\frac{1}{3}$ | | | | $\frac{3}{3}$ |

| $\frac{1}{4}$ | | | $\frac{1}{4}$ | | | $\frac{1}{4}$ | | | $\frac{1}{4}$ | | | $\frac{4}{4}$ |

| $\frac{1}{5}$ | | $\frac{1}{5}$ | | $\frac{1}{5}$ | | $\frac{1}{5}$ | | $\frac{1}{5}$ | | | | $\frac{5}{5}$ |

| $\frac{1}{6}$ | $\frac{1}{6}$ | $\frac{1}{6}$ | $\frac{1}{6}$ | $\frac{1}{6}$ | $\frac{1}{6}$ | | | | | | | $\frac{6}{6}$ |

$\frac{1}{7}$ $\frac{1}{7}$ $\frac{1}{7}$ $\frac{1}{7}$ $\frac{1}{7}$ $\frac{1}{7}$ $\frac{1}{7}$ — $\frac{7}{7}$

$\frac{1}{8}$ $\frac{1}{8}$ $\frac{1}{8}$ $\frac{1}{8}$ $\frac{1}{8}$ $\frac{1}{8}$ $\frac{1}{8}$ $\frac{1}{8}$ — $\frac{8}{8}$

$\frac{1}{9}$ $\frac{1}{9}$ $\frac{1}{9}$ $\frac{1}{9}$ $\frac{1}{9}$ $\frac{1}{9}$ $\frac{1}{9}$ $\frac{1}{9}$ $\frac{1}{9}$ — $\frac{9}{9}$

$\frac{1}{10}$ $\frac{1}{10}$ $\frac{1}{10}$ $\frac{1}{10}$ $\frac{1}{10}$ $\frac{1}{10}$ $\frac{1}{10}$ $\frac{1}{10}$ $\frac{1}{10}$ $\frac{1}{10}$ — $\frac{10}{10}$

$\frac{1}{11}$ $\frac{1}{11}$ $\frac{1}{11}$ $\frac{1}{11}$ $\frac{1}{11}$ $\frac{1}{11}$ $\frac{1}{11}$ $\frac{1}{11}$ $\frac{1}{11}$ $\frac{1}{11}$ $\frac{1}{11}$ — $\frac{11}{11}$

$\frac{1}{12}$ $\frac{1}{12}$ $\frac{1}{12}$ $\frac{1}{12}$ $\frac{1}{12}$ $\frac{1}{12}$ $\frac{1}{12}$ $\frac{1}{12}$ $\frac{1}{12}$ $\frac{1}{12}$ $\frac{1}{12}$ $\frac{1}{12}$ — $\frac{12}{12}$

2. Puzzled Penguin knows that 4 is greater than 2, so he thinks that $\frac{1}{4}$ is greater than $\frac{1}{2}$. Is he right or wrong? Explain.

_____

_____

_____

Class Activity

▶ Practice Comparing Fractions

Circle the greater fraction. Use your fraction strips if you need to.

3. $\frac{1}{12}$ or $\frac{1}{2}$ 4. $\frac{3}{8}$ or $\frac{1}{8}$

5. $\frac{2}{5}$ or $\frac{2}{7}$ 6. $\frac{1}{3}$ or $\frac{1}{5}$

7. $\frac{4}{12}$ or $\frac{5}{12}$ 8. $\frac{7}{9}$ or $\frac{5}{9}$

9. $\frac{1}{7}$ or $\frac{2}{7}$ 10. $\frac{3}{6}$ or $\frac{3}{8}$

Write < or > to make each statement true.

11. $\frac{3}{10}$ $\bigcirc$ $\frac{3}{9}$ 12. $\frac{3}{6}$ $\bigcirc$ $\frac{3}{5}$

13. $\frac{8}{16}$ $\bigcirc$ $\frac{8}{18}$ 14. $\frac{2}{7}$ $\bigcirc$ $\frac{3}{7}$

15. $\frac{7}{15}$ $\bigcirc$ $\frac{7}{14}$ 16. $\frac{5}{11}$ $\bigcirc$ $\frac{4}{11}$

17. Explain how to compare fractions with the same denominator but different numerators.

_____

_____

_____

18. Explain how to compare fractions with the same numerator but different denominators.

_____

_____

_____

$\frac{1}{1}$		$\frac{1}{1}$

| $\frac{1}{2}$ | $\frac{1}{2}$ | $\frac{2}{2}$ |

| $\frac{1}{3}$ | $\frac{1}{3}$ | $\frac{1}{3}$ | $\frac{3}{3}$ |

| $\frac{1}{4}$ | $\frac{1}{4}$ | $\frac{1}{4}$ | $\frac{1}{4}$ | $\frac{4}{4}$ |

| $\frac{1}{5}$ | $\frac{1}{5}$ | $\frac{1}{5}$ | $\frac{1}{5}$ | $\frac{1}{5}$ | $\frac{5}{5}$ |

| $\frac{1}{6}$ | $\frac{1}{6}$ | $\frac{1}{6}$ | $\frac{1}{6}$ | $\frac{1}{6}$ | $\frac{1}{6}$ | $\frac{6}{6}$ |

| $\frac{1}{7}$ | $\frac{1}{7}$ | $\frac{1}{7}$ | $\frac{1}{7}$ | $\frac{1}{7}$ | $\frac{1}{7}$ | $\frac{1}{7}$ | $\frac{7}{7}$ |

| $\frac{1}{8}$ | $\frac{1}{8}$ | $\frac{1}{8}$ | $\frac{1}{8}$ | $\frac{1}{8}$ | $\frac{1}{8}$ | $\frac{1}{8}$ | $\frac{1}{8}$ | $\frac{8}{8}$ |

| $\frac{1}{9}$ | $\frac{1}{9}$ | $\frac{1}{9}$ | $\frac{1}{9}$ | $\frac{1}{9}$ | $\frac{1}{9}$ | $\frac{1}{9}$ | $\frac{1}{9}$ | $\frac{1}{9}$ | $\frac{9}{9}$ |

| $\frac{1}{10}$ | $\frac{1}{10}$ | $\frac{1}{10}$ | $\frac{1}{10}$ | $\frac{1}{10}$ | $\frac{1}{10}$ | $\frac{1}{10}$ | $\frac{1}{10}$ | $\frac{1}{10}$ | $\frac{1}{10}$ | $\frac{10}{10}$ |

| $\frac{1}{11}$ | $\frac{1}{11}$ | $\frac{1}{11}$ | $\frac{1}{11}$ | $\frac{1}{11}$ | $\frac{1}{11}$ | $\frac{1}{11}$ | $\frac{1}{11}$ | $\frac{1}{11}$ | $\frac{1}{11}$ | $\frac{1}{11}$ | $\frac{11}{11}$ |

| $\frac{1}{12}$ | $\frac{1}{12}$ | $\frac{1}{12}$ | $\frac{1}{12}$ | $\frac{1}{12}$ | $\frac{1}{12}$ | $\frac{1}{12}$ | $\frac{1}{12}$ | $\frac{1}{12}$ | $\frac{1}{12}$ | $\frac{1}{12}$ | $\frac{1}{12}$ | $\frac{12}{12}$ |

| $\frac{1}{13}$ | $\frac{1}{13}$ | $\frac{1}{13}$ | $\frac{1}{13}$ | $\frac{1}{13}$ | $\frac{1}{13}$ | $\frac{1}{13}$ | $\frac{1}{13}$ | $\frac{1}{13}$ | $\frac{1}{13}$ | $\frac{1}{13}$ | $\frac{1}{13}$ | $\frac{1}{13}$ | $\frac{13}{13}$ |

| $\frac{1}{14}$ | $\frac{1}{14}$ | $\frac{1}{14}$ | $\frac{1}{14}$ | $\frac{1}{14}$ | $\frac{1}{14}$ | $\frac{1}{14}$ | $\frac{1}{14}$ | $\frac{1}{14}$ | $\frac{1}{14}$ | $\frac{1}{14}$ | $\frac{1}{14}$ | $\frac{1}{14}$ | $\frac{1}{14}$ | $\frac{14}{14}$ |

| $\frac{1}{15}$ | $\frac{1}{15}$ | $\frac{1}{15}$ | $\frac{1}{15}$ | $\frac{1}{15}$ | $\frac{1}{15}$ | $\frac{1}{15}$ | $\frac{1}{15}$ | $\frac{1}{15}$ | $\frac{1}{15}$ | $\frac{1}{15}$ | $\frac{1}{15}$ | $\frac{1}{15}$ | $\frac{1}{15}$ | $\frac{1}{15}$ | $\frac{15}{15}$ |

| $\frac{1}{16}$ | $\frac{1}{16}$ | $\frac{1}{16}$ | $\frac{1}{16}$ | $\frac{1}{16}$ | $\frac{1}{16}$ | $\frac{1}{16}$ | $\frac{1}{16}$ | $\frac{1}{16}$ | $\frac{1}{16}$ | $\frac{1}{16}$ | $\frac{1}{16}$ | $\frac{1}{16}$ | $\frac{1}{16}$ | $\frac{1}{16}$ | $\frac{1}{16}$ | $\frac{16}{16}$ |

| $\frac{1}{17}$ | $\frac{1}{17}$ | $\frac{1}{17}$ | $\frac{1}{17}$ | $\frac{1}{17}$ | $\frac{1}{17}$ | $\frac{1}{17}$ | $\frac{1}{17}$ | $\frac{1}{17}$ | $\frac{1}{17}$ | $\frac{1}{17}$ | $\frac{1}{17}$ | $\frac{1}{17}$ | $\frac{1}{17}$ | $\frac{1}{17}$ | $\frac{1}{17}$ | $\frac{1}{17}$ | $\frac{17}{17}$ |

| $\frac{1}{18}$ | $\frac{1}{18}$ | $\frac{1}{18}$ | $\frac{1}{18}$ | $\frac{1}{18}$ | $\frac{1}{18}$ | $\frac{1}{18}$ | $\frac{1}{18}$ | $\frac{1}{18}$ | $\frac{1}{18}$ | $\frac{1}{18}$ | $\frac{1}{18}$ | $\frac{1}{18}$ | $\frac{1}{18}$ | $\frac{1}{18}$ | $\frac{1}{18}$ | $\frac{1}{18}$ | $\frac{1}{18}$ | $\frac{18}{18}$ |

| $\frac{1}{19}$ | $\frac{1}{19}$ | $\frac{1}{19}$ | $\frac{1}{19}$ | $\frac{1}{19}$ | $\frac{1}{19}$ | $\frac{1}{19}$ | $\frac{1}{19}$ | $\frac{1}{19}$ | $\frac{1}{19}$ | $\frac{1}{19}$ | $\frac{1}{19}$ | $\frac{1}{19}$ | $\frac{1}{19}$ | $\frac{1}{19}$ | $\frac{1}{19}$ | $\frac{1}{19}$ | $\frac{1}{19}$ | $\frac{1}{19}$ | $\frac{19}{19}$ |

| $\frac{1}{20}$ | $\frac{1}{20}$ | $\frac{1}{20}$ | $\frac{1}{20}$ | $\frac{1}{20}$ | $\frac{1}{20}$ | $\frac{1}{20}$ | $\frac{1}{20}$ | $\frac{1}{20}$ | $\frac{1}{20}$ | $\frac{1}{20}$ | $\frac{1}{20}$ | $\frac{1}{20}$ | $\frac{1}{20}$ | $\frac{1}{20}$ | $\frac{1}{20}$ | $\frac{1}{20}$ | $\frac{1}{20}$ | $\frac{1}{20}$ | $\frac{1}{20}$ | $\frac{20}{20}$ |

► Compare Fractions of Different-Size Wholes

Jon and his five friends want sandwiches. They make two different kinds: one on a short loaf of bread and one on a longer loaf. Jon cuts each sandwich into 6 pieces. His friends think the pieces are not the same size.

1. Are Jon's friends correct? Explain.

_____

_____

_____

2. What can Jon do to make sure everyone gets the same amount of food?

_____

_____

Hattie's dad orders one small, one medium, and one large pizza. He divides each pizza into 8 equal pieces. Hattie takes $\frac{1}{8}$ of the small pizza and her friend takes $\frac{1}{8}$ of the large pizza.

 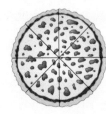 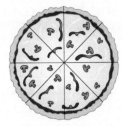

3. Hattie says she has less pizza than her friend. Is she correct? Explain.

_____

_____

_____

4. What do these problems tell us about fractions?

_____

▶ Fraction Word Problems

Solve.

5. A shelter had 4 spaniel puppies and 6 beagle puppies. Jack adopted $\frac{1}{2}$ of the spaniel puppies, and Carmen adopted $\frac{1}{2}$ of the beagle puppies. Who adopted more puppies? How do you know?

_____

_____

6. Julio planted 16 daisies and 10 sunflowers. His neighbor's goat ate 5 daisies and 5 sunflowers. Did the goat eat a larger fractional part of the daisies or the sunflowers? Explain.

_____

_____

_____

_____

7. A fruit market sells two different packages of oranges. Bags contain 12 oranges, and boxes contain 15 oranges. Both packages cost $3.00. Which package is a better buy? Why?

_____

_____

8. The fourth grade has three running teams. Each team has 12 runners. In a race, $\frac{1}{4}$ of Team A, $\frac{1}{3}$ of Team B, and $\frac{1}{6}$ of Team C passed the first water stop at the same time. Which team had the most runners at the first water stop at that time? Explain.

_____

_____

▶ **Compare Polygons and Circles**

Name each regular polygon.

1.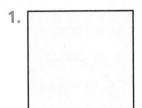

2.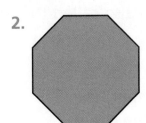

3.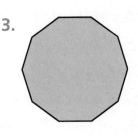

4.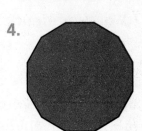

_____   _____   _____   _____

5. What happens to the angles of regular polygons as they have more and more sides?

_____

_____

6. What is the name of a smooth curved line around the outside of a regular polygon everywhere equidistant from the center?

_____

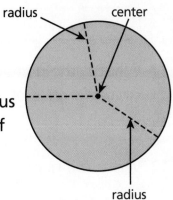

▶ **Radius and Diameter**

A line segment joining the **center** of a circle to any point on its perimeter is called a **radius**. For any circle, every radius has the same length. That length is also called the radius of the circle. A line segment drawn through the center of a circle is called its **diameter**. Its length is also called the diameter of the circle.

radius   center

radius

7. What is the radius of this circle? _____

8. What is the diameter? _____

9. How can knowing about radius help you draw a circle?

_____

_____

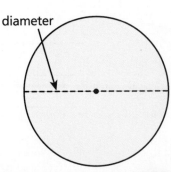

diameter

Vocabulary

circumference
pi

▶ Explore Circumference

The curved line around the edge or perimeter of a circle is its **circumference**. The length of that line is also called the circumference of the circle.

If you divide the circumference (*C*) of a circle by its diameter (*d*), you always get the same number. The number is called **pi**, and it is written with the Greek letter π.

Pi is about 3.14 or $\frac{22}{7}$.

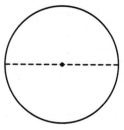

$$C \div d = \pi$$

10. If you know the product and one factor of any division, how can you find the other factor? $\frac{C}{d} = \pi$

_____

_____

11. If you know the diameter of a circle and you know π, how can you find the circumference of the circle?

_____

_____

12. What is the general equation for finding the circumference of a circle?

$$C = \text{_____}$$

13. Write the name of each part of the circle.

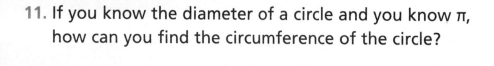

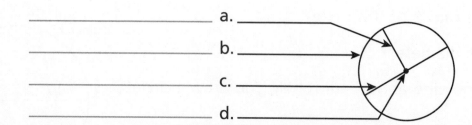

_____ a. _____

_____ b. _____

_____ c. _____

_____ d. _____

Circles

Name _____ Date _____

▶ Divide a Circle

We can divide a whole circle into equal parts. We can show this with a round pizza.

What part of the whole pizza does one slice show?

1.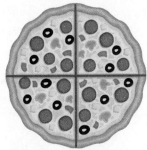

2.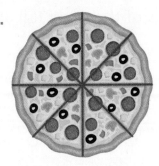

3.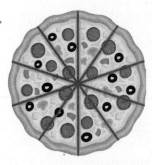

_____ _____ _____

Mark the largest part with an L and the smallest part with an S. Place a check mark (✓) beside the parts of equal size.

4.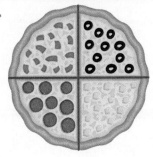

5.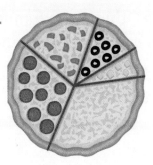

6.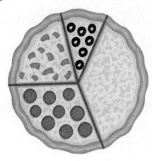

7. How can you tell the relative sizes of the parts of the pizzas in exercises 5 and 6?

_____

_____

_____

_____

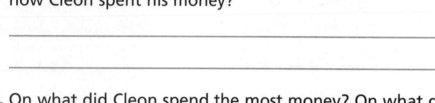

▶ Read Circle Graphs

A **circle graph** can show parts of any kind of whole.

Cleon gets $10.00 from his parents each week. The circle graph shows how Cleon spent his money last week.

8. What do the sizes of the parts of the circle tell about how Cleon spent his money?

_____

_____

Money Spent Last Week

9. On what did Cleon spend the most money? On what did he spend the least money? How do you know?

_____

_____

_____

10. If Cleon spent $1.00 on "Other" things, how much did he probably spend on lunches at school? Explain your thinking.

_____

_____

_____

11. How much did Cleon probably spend on snacks last week?

_____

12. What is probably the most Cleon could have spent to go to the school movie night with his friends last week?

_____

Explore Circle Graphs

Name _____   **Date** _____

► Compare Circle Graphs

You can use a circle graph to compare parts of equal-sized wholes.

The circle graph to the right shows how Cleon spent his $10.00 this week.

Money Spent Last Week

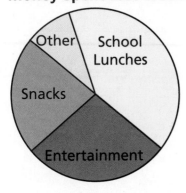

Money Spent This Week

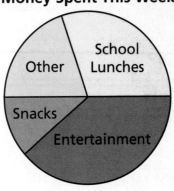

13. What is the whole for both circle graphs?

_____

14. How much did Cleon spend this week on School Lunches? on Snacks? on Other?

_____

15. On what did Cleon spend more this week than last week? On what did he spend less? Explain how you know.

_____

_____

_____

_____

16. How much could Cleon have spent on a computer game this week?

_____

Name _____

Date _____

Going Further

► Circle Graphs Showing Percents

Circle graphs are a good way to show percents because the circle represents one whole, or 100%.

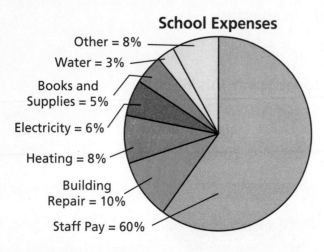

School Expenses

Other = 8%
Water = 3%
Books and Supplies = 5%
Electricity = 6%
Heating = 8%
Building Repair = 10%
Staff Pay = 60%

17. What information does the graph give?

_____

18. What information doesn't it give?

_____

19. What is the largest expense for the school?

_____

20. Which expense costs the school 5% of its budget?

_____

21. Does the school spend more on Heating or on Water?

_____

22. What is the difference in percents between Heating and Water?

_____

23. Write two more questions about the circle graph.

_____

Explore Circle Graphs

Name _____ **Date** _____

Class Activity

▶ Add and Subtract Fractions

The circled parts of this fraction bar show an addition problem.

| $\frac{1}{7}$ | $\frac{1}{7}$ | $\frac{1}{7}$ | $\frac{1}{7}$ | $\frac{1}{7}$ | $\frac{1}{7}$ | $\frac{1}{7}$ |

1. Write the numerators that will complete the addition equation.

$$\frac{}{7} + \frac{}{7} = \frac{ + }{7} = \frac{}{7}$$

Solve each problem. Write the correct numerator to complete each equation.

2. $\dfrac{3}{9} + \dfrac{4}{9} = \dfrac{ + }{9} = \dfrac{}{9}$ 3. $\dfrac{1}{5} + \dfrac{3}{5} = \dfrac{ + }{5} = \dfrac{}{5}$ 4. $\dfrac{2}{8} + \dfrac{5}{8} = \dfrac{ + }{8} = \dfrac{}{8}$

5. What happens to the numerators in each problem?

_____

6. What happens to the denominators in each problem?

_____

The circled and crossed-out parts of this fraction bar show a subtraction problem.

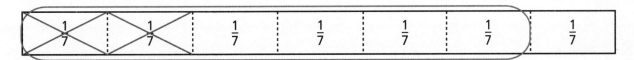

7. Write the numerators that will complete the subtraction equation.

$$\frac{}{7} - \frac{}{7} = \frac{ - }{7} = \frac{}{7}$$

► Add and Subtract Fractions (continued)

Solve each problem. Write the correct numerators to complete each sentence.

8. $\dfrac{5}{6} - \dfrac{4}{6} = \dfrac{—}{6} = \dfrac{}{6}$

9. $\dfrac{9}{10} - \dfrac{5}{10} = \dfrac{—}{10} = —$

10. $\dfrac{14}{16} - \dfrac{9}{16} = \dfrac{—}{16} = —$

11. What happens to the numerators in each problem?

_____

12. How is subtraction of fractions with like denominators
    similar to addition of fractions with like denominators?

_____

_____

► Mixed Practice With Addition and Subtraction

Puzzled Penguin knows that if he catches 3 fish and then
catches 2 more fish, he has 5 fish. He also knows that if he
catches 4 fish and eats 3 of his fish, he has 1 fish left.
This is what he wrote:

$\dfrac{3}{5} + \dfrac{2}{5} = \dfrac{5}{10}$ $\dfrac{4}{5} - \dfrac{3}{5} = \dfrac{1}{0}$

13. What part of his work is not correct? _____

14. What can you tell him that will help him understand how to add and
    subtract fractions with like denominators properly? _____

_____

_____

Solve each problem. Include the "circled" step in 18–23.

15. $\dfrac{1}{4} + \dfrac{2}{4} = \left(\dfrac{+}{4}\right) =$

16. $\dfrac{3}{9} + \dfrac{5}{9} = \left(\dfrac{+}{9}\right) =$

17. $\dfrac{12}{6} - \dfrac{2}{6} = \left(\dfrac{-}{6}\right) =$

18. $\dfrac{4}{10} + \dfrac{5}{10} =$

19. $\dfrac{2}{5} + \dfrac{4}{5} =$

20. $\dfrac{8}{12} - \dfrac{3}{12} =$

21. $\dfrac{5}{7} + \dfrac{3}{7} =$

22. $\dfrac{7}{11} - \dfrac{4}{11} =$

23. $\dfrac{9}{8} - \dfrac{5}{8} =$

Class Activity

Name _____ **Date** _____

▶ Work With Unit Fractions

| one whole | $\frac{1}{1}$ |

| $\frac{1}{2}$ | $\frac{1}{2}$ | $\frac{2}{2}$ |

| $\frac{1}{3}$ | $\frac{1}{3}$ | $\frac{1}{3}$ | $\frac{3}{3}$ |

| $\frac{1}{4}$ | $\frac{1}{4}$ | $\frac{1}{4}$ | $\frac{1}{4}$ | $\frac{4}{4}$ |

| $\frac{1}{5}$ | $\frac{1}{5}$ | $\frac{1}{5}$ | $\frac{1}{5}$ | $\frac{1}{5}$ | $\frac{5}{5}$ |

| $\frac{1}{6}$ | $\frac{1}{6}$ | $\frac{1}{6}$ | $\frac{1}{6}$ | $\frac{1}{6}$ | $\frac{1}{6}$ | $\frac{6}{6}$ |

| $\frac{1}{7}$ | $\frac{1}{7}$ | $\frac{1}{7}$ | $\frac{1}{7}$ | $\frac{1}{7}$ | $\frac{1}{7}$ | $\frac{1}{7}$ | $\frac{7}{7}$ |

| $\frac{1}{8}$ | $\frac{1}{8}$ | $\frac{1}{8}$ | $\frac{1}{8}$ | $\frac{1}{8}$ | $\frac{1}{8}$ | $\frac{1}{8}$ | $\frac{1}{8}$ | $\frac{8}{8}$ |

| $\frac{1}{9}$ | $\frac{1}{9}$ | $\frac{1}{9}$ | $\frac{1}{9}$ | $\frac{1}{9}$ | $\frac{1}{9}$ | $\frac{1}{9}$ | $\frac{1}{9}$ | $\frac{1}{9}$ | $\frac{9}{9}$ |

| $\frac{1}{10}$ | $\frac{1}{10}$ | $\frac{1}{10}$ | $\frac{1}{10}$ | $\frac{1}{10}$ | $\frac{1}{10}$ | $\frac{1}{10}$ | $\frac{1}{10}$ | $\frac{1}{10}$ | $\frac{1}{10}$ | $\frac{10}{10}$ |

| $\frac{1}{12}$ | $\frac{1}{12}$ | $\frac{1}{12}$ | $\frac{1}{12}$ | $\frac{1}{12}$ | $\frac{1}{12}$ | $\frac{1}{12}$ | $\frac{1}{12}$ | $\frac{1}{12}$ | $\frac{1}{12}$ | $\frac{1}{12}$ | $\frac{1}{12}$ | $\frac{12}{12}$ |

Vocabulary
improper fraction
mixed number

► Discuss Real-World Uses of Mixed Numbers

Mellie's Deli makes sandwiches. This is the price list.

Mellie's Deli

Regular (serves 2) _____ $3.00
Friendship (serves 4) _____ $5.00
Super (serves 10) _____ $12.00
Magna (serves 18)_____ $20.00

Nineteen friends decide to camp in the park. They order two Super sandwiches. Each camper eats 1 serving.

Solve.

1. How many campers does one Super sandwich serve?

   _____

2. What fraction of the second sandwich is needed to serve the rest of the campers?

   _____

3. What fraction of the second sandwich is left over?

   _____

4. What number tells how many Super sandwiches the campers ate in all?

   _____

► Define Mixed Number and Improper Fraction

An **improper fraction** is a fraction that has a numerator greater than or equal to its denominator.	$\frac{10}{6}$ $\frac{19}{5}$ $\frac{3}{3}$
A **mixed number** is a number that consists of a whole number and a fraction.	$1\frac{4}{6}$ $3\frac{4}{5}$

▶ Convert Between Mixed Numbers and Improper Fractions

Change each mixed number to an improper fraction and each improper fraction to a mixed number.

5. $5\frac{2}{3} =$

6. $3\frac{3}{7} =$

7. $6\frac{6}{10} =$

8. $9\frac{1}{4} =$

9. $2\frac{7}{8} =$

10. $4\frac{5}{9} =$

11. $8\frac{3}{5} =$

12. $7\frac{4}{6} =$

13. $\frac{40}{6} =$

14. $\frac{11}{2} =$

15. $\frac{23}{7} =$

16. $\frac{28}{3} =$

17. $\frac{22}{4} =$

18. $\frac{25}{8} =$

19. $\frac{29}{7} =$

20. $6\frac{4}{8} =$

21. $4\frac{6}{9} =$

22. $\frac{16}{3} =$

▶ Fraction Strips

1 whole

$\frac{1}{8}$	$\frac{1}{8}$	$\frac{1}{8}$	$\frac{1}{8}$	$\frac{1}{8}$	$\frac{1}{8}$	$\frac{1}{8}$	$\frac{1}{8}$
$\frac{1}{8}$	$\frac{1}{8}$	$\frac{1}{8}$	$\frac{1}{8}$	$\frac{1}{8}$	$\frac{1}{8}$	$\frac{1}{8}$	$\frac{1}{8}$
$\frac{1}{8}$	$\frac{1}{8}$	$\frac{1}{8}$	$\frac{1}{8}$	$\frac{1}{8}$	$\frac{1}{8}$	$\frac{1}{8}$	$\frac{1}{8}$
$\frac{1}{8}$	$\frac{1}{8}$	$\frac{1}{8}$	$\frac{1}{8}$	$\frac{1}{8}$	$\frac{1}{8}$	$\frac{1}{8}$	$\frac{1}{8}$
$\frac{1}{8}$	$\frac{1}{8}$	$\frac{1}{8}$	$\frac{1}{8}$	$\frac{1}{8}$	$\frac{1}{8}$	$\frac{1}{8}$	$\frac{1}{8}$
$\frac{1}{8}$	$\frac{1}{8}$	$\frac{1}{8}$	$\frac{1}{8}$	$\frac{1}{8}$	$\frac{1}{8}$	$\frac{1}{8}$	$\frac{1}{8}$
$\frac{1}{8}$	$\frac{1}{8}$	$\frac{1}{8}$	$\frac{1}{8}$	$\frac{1}{8}$	$\frac{1}{8}$	$\frac{1}{8}$	$\frac{1}{8}$

$\frac{1}{5}$	$\frac{1}{5}$	$\frac{1}{5}$	$\frac{1}{5}$	$\frac{1}{5}$
$\frac{1}{5}$	$\frac{1}{5}$	$\frac{1}{5}$	$\frac{1}{5}$	$\frac{1}{5}$
$\frac{1}{5}$	$\frac{1}{5}$	$\frac{1}{5}$	$\frac{1}{5}$	$\frac{1}{5}$
$\frac{1}{5}$	$\frac{1}{5}$	$\frac{1}{5}$	$\frac{1}{5}$	$\frac{1}{5}$
$\frac{1}{5}$	$\frac{1}{5}$	$\frac{1}{5}$	$\frac{1}{5}$	$\frac{1}{5}$
$\frac{1}{5}$	$\frac{1}{5}$	$\frac{1}{5}$	$\frac{1}{5}$	$\frac{1}{5}$
$\frac{1}{5}$	$\frac{1}{5}$	$\frac{1}{5}$	$\frac{1}{5}$	$\frac{1}{5}$

1 whole

1 whole
1 whole
1 whole
1 whole
1 whole
1 whole
1 whole

1 whole
1 whole
1 whole
1 whole
1 whole
1 whole
1 whole

Name _____   Date _____

▶ Practice Addition and Subtraction With Improper Fractions

Add or subtract.

1. $\dfrac{8}{5} + \dfrac{3}{5} =$ _____

2. $\dfrac{6}{9} + \dfrac{12}{9} =$ _____

3. $\dfrac{10}{7} - \dfrac{3}{7} =$ _____

4. $\dfrac{10}{8} + \dfrac{7}{8} =$ _____

5. $\dfrac{9}{6} - \dfrac{4}{6} =$ _____

6. $\dfrac{16}{10} - \dfrac{7}{10} =$ _____

▶ Add Mixed Numbers With Like Denominators

Add.

7.
$$2\tfrac{3}{5}$$
$$+\ 1\tfrac{1}{5}$$

8.
$$1\tfrac{2}{5}$$
$$+\ 3\tfrac{4}{5}$$

9.
$$3\tfrac{5}{8}$$
$$+\ 1\tfrac{3}{8}$$

10.
$$5\tfrac{2}{3}$$
$$+\ 2\tfrac{2}{3}$$

▶ Subtract Mixed Numbers With Like Denominators

Subtract.

11.
$$5\tfrac{6}{8}$$
$$-\ 3\tfrac{3}{8}$$

12.
$$6\tfrac{2}{8}$$
$$-\ 4\tfrac{5}{8}$$

13.
$$4\tfrac{1}{5}$$
$$-\ 1\tfrac{3}{5}$$

14.
$$5\tfrac{1}{6}$$
$$-\ 3\tfrac{4}{6}$$

Explain each solution.

15.
$$\overset{7+2=9}{\cancel{6}\tfrac{2}{7}} = 5\tfrac{9}{7}$$
$$-\ 1\tfrac{5}{7} = 1\tfrac{5}{7}$$
$$\overline{\qquad 4\tfrac{4}{7}}$$

16.
$$\overset{6+2=8}{\cancel{6}\tfrac{2}{6}} = 5\tfrac{8}{6}$$
$$-\ 1\tfrac{5}{6} = 1\tfrac{5}{6}$$
$$\overline{\qquad 4\tfrac{3}{6}}$$

17.
$$\overset{11+2=13}{\cancel{6}\tfrac{2}{11}} = 5\tfrac{13}{11}$$
$$-\ 1\tfrac{5}{11} = 1\tfrac{5}{11}$$
$$\overline{\qquad 4\tfrac{8}{11}}$$

_____

_____

_____

Class Activity

▶ Puzzled Penguin

Dear Math Students:

Here is a subtraction problem that I tried to solve.

$$\begin{array}{r} 7\frac{3}{8} \\ -\ 1\frac{5}{8} \\ \hline 6\frac{2}{8} \end{array}$$

Is my answer correct? If not, please help me understand why it is wrong.

Thank you,
Puzzled Penguin

18. _____

_____

_____

▶ Compare and Subtract

Compare each pair of mixed numbers. Then subtract the smaller one from the larger.

19. $3\frac{2}{5}$; $1\frac{4}{5}$ _____

20. $\frac{8}{9}$; $2\frac{2}{9}$ _____

21. $\frac{14}{11}$; $1\frac{6}{11}$ _____

22. $4\frac{1}{8}$; $2\frac{7}{8}$ _____

23. $3\frac{2}{6}$; $4\frac{3}{6}$ _____

24. $10\frac{1}{3}$; $7\frac{2}{3}$ _____

Add and Subtract Mixed Numbers With Like Denominators

▶ Compare, Add, and Subtract Fractions

Practice what you know.

Circle the greater fraction.

1. $\frac{4}{6}$ or $\frac{4}{5}$

2. $\frac{8}{10}$ or $\frac{7}{10}$

3. $\frac{6}{9}$ or $\frac{6}{10}$

4. $\frac{2}{3}$ or $\frac{2}{4}$

5. $\frac{5}{7}$ or $\frac{5}{8}$

6. $\frac{7}{8}$ or $\frac{6}{8}$

Compare each pair of fractions. Then add them to find the total and subtract the smaller one from the larger one to find the difference.

7. $\frac{6}{10}, \frac{3}{10}$ _____

8. $\frac{4}{6}, \frac{5}{6}$ _____

9. $\frac{2}{7}, \frac{5}{7}$ _____

10. $\frac{4}{5}, \frac{2}{5}$ _____

11. $\frac{7}{9}, \frac{3}{9}$ _____

12. $\frac{7}{8}, \frac{4}{8}$ _____

Add or subtract.

13. $\frac{3}{6} + \frac{2}{6} =$ _____

14. $\frac{4}{7} + \frac{1}{7} =$ _____

15. $\frac{5}{8} - \frac{4}{8} =$ _____

16. $\frac{4}{9} + \frac{4}{9} =$ _____

17. $\frac{3}{4} - \frac{2}{4} =$ _____

18. $\frac{8}{10} - \frac{3}{10} =$ _____

Compare each pair of mixed numbers. Then find the total and the difference.

19. $2\frac{3}{4}, 3\frac{1}{4}$ _____

20. $1\frac{5}{12}, 5\frac{3}{12}$ _____

▶ **On the Back** Write four improper fractions. Write each one as a mixed number. Write four mixed numbers. Write each one as an improper fraction.

Practice With Fractions

▶ Equivalent Fractions

Read and discuss the problem situation.

Luis works summers at Maria's Fruit Farm. One day, Maria agreed to give Luis extra pay if he could sell $\frac{2}{3}$ of her supply of peaches. They started with 15 bags of peaches, and Luis sold 10 of them.

1. Luis said to Maria, "Ten bags is $\frac{10}{15}$ of the 15 bags you wanted to sell. I think $\frac{2}{3}$ is the same as $\frac{10}{15}$. I can show you why." Luis made this drawing. Did Luis earn his pay?

| $\frac{1}{15}$ | $\frac{1}{15}$ | $\frac{1}{15}$ | $\frac{1}{15}$ | $\frac{1}{15}$ | $\frac{1}{15}$ | $\frac{1}{15}$ | $\frac{1}{15}$ | $\frac{1}{15}$ | $\frac{1}{15}$ | $\frac{1}{15}$ | $\frac{1}{15}$ | $\frac{1}{15}$ | $\frac{1}{15}$ | $\frac{1}{15}$ |

| $\frac{1}{3}$ | $\frac{1}{3}$ | $\frac{1}{3}$ |

$$\frac{5}{15} \qquad + \qquad \frac{5}{15} \qquad \qquad \frac{5}{15}$$

$$\frac{1}{3} \qquad + \qquad \frac{1}{3} \qquad \qquad \frac{1}{3}$$

$$\underbrace{\qquad\qquad\qquad\qquad}_{\frac{10}{15} = \frac{2}{3}}$$

2. Maria said, "You are just making groups of 5 fifteenths. You can show what you did using numbers." Here's what Maria wrote:

$$\frac{10}{15} = \frac{10 \div 5}{15 \div 5} = \frac{2}{3}$$

Discuss what Maria did. How does dividing the numerator and denominator by 5 affect the fraction?

Vocabulary

equivalent fractions
simplify
simplest form

▶ Simplify Fractions

Two fractions that represent the same part of a whole are **equivalent fractions**. The fractions $\frac{10}{15}$ and $\frac{2}{3}$ are equivalent.

Simplifying a fraction means finding an equivalent fraction with a smaller numerator and denominator.

A fraction is in **simplest form** if there is no whole number (other than 1) that divides evenly into both the numerator and denominator.

3. Maria had 12 boxes of apricots. She sold 10 of the boxes. Write the fraction of the boxes sold, and lightly shade the twelfths fraction bar to show this fraction.

Fraction sold: _____

4. Group the twelfths to form an equivalent fraction with a smaller denominator. Show the new fraction by dividing, labeling, and lightly shading the blank fraction bar.

Fraction sold: _____

$\frac{1}{12}$	$\frac{1}{12}$	$\frac{1}{12}$	$\frac{1}{12}$	$\frac{1}{12}$	$\frac{1}{12}$	$\frac{1}{12}$	$\frac{1}{12}$	$\frac{1}{12}$	$\frac{1}{12}$	$\frac{1}{12}$	$\frac{1}{12}$

5. In problem 4, you formed groups of twelfths to get a larger unit fraction. How many twelfths are in each group? In other words, what is the *group size*?

_____

6. Show how you can find the equivalent fraction by dividing the numerator and denominator by the group size.

$$\frac{10}{12} = \frac{10 \div \Box}{12 \div \Box} = \frac{\Box}{\Box}$$

Use what you know to find these equivalent fractions. You may want to sketch a thirds fraction bar below the two fraction bars above.

7. $\frac{8}{12} = \frac{\Box}{6} = \frac{\Box}{3}$

8. $\frac{4}{12} = \frac{\Box}{6} = \frac{\Box}{3}$

9. $\frac{20}{12} = \frac{\Box}{6} = \frac{\Box}{3} = \Box\frac{\Box}{3}$

▶ Simplify Fractions (continued)

Shade the bar to show the fraction of items sold. Group the unit fractions to form an equivalent fraction in simplest form. Show your work numerically.

10. Maria had 12 bags of grapes. She sold 9 bags.
What fraction did she sell?

| $\frac{1}{12}$ | $\frac{1}{12}$ | $\frac{1}{12}$ | $\frac{1}{12}$ | $\frac{1}{12}$ | $\frac{1}{12}$ | $\frac{1}{12}$ | $\frac{1}{12}$ | $\frac{1}{12}$ | $\frac{1}{12}$ | $\frac{1}{12}$ | $\frac{1}{12}$ |

Group size: _____

Fraction of bags sold: $\dfrac{9 \div}{12 \div} = \underline{}$

11. Maria had 15 crates of apples. She sold 6 crates.
What fraction did she sell?

| $\frac{1}{15}$ | $\frac{1}{15}$ | $\frac{1}{15}$ | $\frac{1}{15}$ | $\frac{1}{15}$ | $\frac{1}{15}$ | $\frac{1}{15}$ | $\frac{1}{15}$ | $\frac{1}{15}$ | $\frac{1}{15}$ | $\frac{1}{15}$ | $\frac{1}{15}$ | $\frac{1}{15}$ | $\frac{1}{15}$ | $\frac{1}{15}$ |

Group size: _____

Fraction of crates sold: $\dfrac{6 \div}{15 \div} = \underline{}$

12. Maria had 16 jars of cherry jam. She sold 10 jars.
What fraction did she sell?

| $\frac{1}{16}$ | $\frac{1}{16}$ | $\frac{1}{16}$ | $\frac{1}{16}$ | $\frac{1}{16}$ | $\frac{1}{16}$ | $\frac{1}{16}$ | $\frac{1}{16}$ | $\frac{1}{16}$ | $\frac{1}{16}$ | $\frac{1}{16}$ | $\frac{1}{16}$ | $\frac{1}{16}$ | $\frac{1}{16}$ | $\frac{1}{16}$ | $\frac{1}{16}$ |

Group size: _____

Fraction of jars sold: $\dfrac{10 \div}{16 \div} = \underline{}$

13. Maria had 10 packages of pecans. She sold 8 packages.
What fraction did she sell?

| $\frac{1}{10}$ | $\frac{1}{10}$ | $\frac{1}{10}$ | $\frac{1}{10}$ | $\frac{1}{10}$ | $\frac{1}{10}$ | $\frac{1}{10}$ | $\frac{1}{10}$ | $\frac{1}{10}$ | $\frac{1}{10}$ |

Group size: _____

Fraction of packages sold: $\dfrac{8 \div}{10 \div} = \underline{}$

Name	Date

▶ Use Fraction Bars to Find Equivalent Fractions

14. Look at the thirds bar. Circle enough unit fractions on each of the other bars to equal $\frac{1}{3}$.

| $\frac{1}{18}$ | $\frac{1}{18}$ | $\frac{1}{18}$ | $\frac{1}{18}$ | $\frac{1}{18}$ | $\frac{1}{18}$ | $\frac{1}{18}$ | $\frac{1}{18}$ | $\frac{1}{18}$ | $\frac{1}{18}$ | $\frac{1}{18}$ | $\frac{1}{18}$ | $\frac{1}{18}$ | $\frac{1}{18}$ | $\frac{1}{18}$ | $\frac{1}{18}$ | $\frac{1}{18}$ | $\frac{1}{18}$ |

| $\frac{1}{15}$ | $\frac{1}{15}$ | $\frac{1}{15}$ | $\frac{1}{15}$ | $\frac{1}{15}$ | $\frac{1}{15}$ | $\frac{1}{15}$ | $\frac{1}{15}$ | $\frac{1}{15}$ | $\frac{1}{15}$ | $\frac{1}{15}$ | $\frac{1}{15}$ | $\frac{1}{15}$ | $\frac{1}{15}$ | $\frac{1}{15}$ |

| $\frac{1}{12}$ | $\frac{1}{12}$ | $\frac{1}{12}$ | $\frac{1}{12}$ | $\frac{1}{12}$ | $\frac{1}{12}$ | $\frac{1}{12}$ | $\frac{1}{12}$ | $\frac{1}{12}$ | $\frac{1}{12}$ | $\frac{1}{12}$ | $\frac{1}{12}$ |

| $\frac{1}{9}$ | $\frac{1}{9}$ | $\frac{1}{9}$ | $\frac{1}{9}$ | $\frac{1}{9}$ | $\frac{1}{9}$ | $\frac{1}{9}$ | $\frac{1}{9}$ | $\frac{1}{9}$ |

| $\frac{1}{6}$ | $\frac{1}{6}$ | $\frac{1}{6}$ | $\frac{1}{6}$ | $\frac{1}{6}$ | $\frac{1}{6}$ |

| $\frac{1}{3}$ | $\frac{1}{3}$ | $\frac{1}{3}$ |

15. Discuss how the parts of the fraction bars you circled show this fraction chain. Explain how each different group of unit fractions is equal to $\frac{1}{3}$.

$$\frac{6}{18} = \frac{5}{15} = \frac{4}{12} = \frac{3}{9} = \frac{2}{6} = \frac{1}{3}$$

_____

_____

16. Write the group size for each fraction in the fraction chain. The first one is done for you.

____6____   _____   _____   _____   _____   _____

17. Complete each equation by showing how you use group size to simplify. The first is done for you.

$$\frac{6 \div 6}{18 \div 6} = \frac{1}{3} \qquad \frac{5 \div}{15 \div} = \frac{1}{3} \qquad \frac{4 \div}{12 \div} = \frac{1}{3}$$

$$\frac{3 \div}{9 \div} = \frac{1}{3} \qquad \frac{2 \div}{6 \div} = \frac{1}{3}$$

Simplify Fractions

► Use a Multiplication Table to Find Equivalent Fractions

The table on the right shows part of the multiplication table at the left. You can make a chain of fractions equivalent to $\frac{1}{3}$ by using the products in the rows for the factors 1 and 3.

×	1	2	3	4	5	6	7	8	9	10
1	1	2	3	4	5	6	7	8	9	10
2	2	4	6	8	10	12	14	16	18	20
3	3	6	9	12	15	18	21	24	27	30
4	4	8	12	16	20	24	28	32	36	40
5	5	10	15	20	25	30	35	40	45	50
6	6	12	18	24	30	36	42	48	54	60
7	7	14	21	28	35	42	49	56	63	70
8	8	16	24	32	40	48	56	64	72	80
9	9	18	27	36	45	54	63	72	81	90
10	10	20	30	40	50	60	70	80	90	100

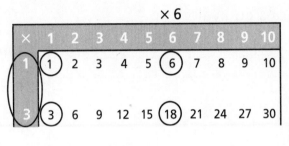

$$\frac{1 \times 6}{3 \times 6} = \frac{6}{18}$$

$$\frac{6 \div 6}{18 \div 6} = \frac{1}{3}$$

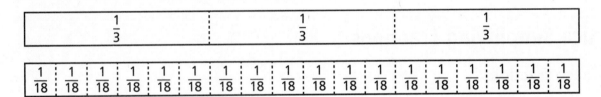

Complete each fraction equation. Look in the top row of the table above to find the multiplier or the divider.

18. $\dfrac{1 \times}{3 \times} = \dfrac{4}{12}$ 19. $\dfrac{1 \times}{3 \times} = \dfrac{9}{27}$ 20. $\dfrac{1 \times}{3 \times} = \dfrac{2}{6}$

21. $\dfrac{8 \div}{24 \div} = \dfrac{1}{3}$ 22. $\dfrac{10 \div}{30 \div} = \dfrac{1}{3}$ 23. $\dfrac{4 \div}{12 \div} = \dfrac{1}{3}$

▶ Use a Multiplication Table to Find Equivalent Fractions (continued)

Here are two more rows from the multiplication table moved together. These rows can be used to generate a chain of fractions equivalent to $\frac{4}{7}$.

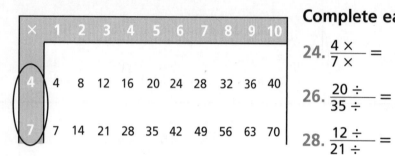

Complete each equation.

24. $\dfrac{4 \times}{7 \times} =$ 　　　　　25. $\dfrac{4 \times}{7 \times} =$

26. $\dfrac{20 \div}{35 \div} =$ 　　　　　27. $\dfrac{36 \div}{63 \div} =$

28. $\dfrac{12 \div}{21 \div} =$ 　　　　　29. $\dfrac{24 \div}{42 \div} =$

Complete each fraction chain.

30. $\dfrac{1}{2} = \dfrac{}{4} = \dfrac{}{8}$ 　　　　31. $\dfrac{}{5} = \dfrac{}{10} = \dfrac{}{20}$

32. $\dfrac{}{3} = \dfrac{}{6} = \dfrac{}{12}$ 　　　　33. $\dfrac{}{2} = \dfrac{}{4} = \dfrac{}{8}$

▶ Practice Simplifying Fractions

Simplify each fraction.

34. $\dfrac{4 \div}{20 \div} =$ 　　　　　35. $\dfrac{14 \div}{35 \div} =$

36. $\dfrac{3 \div}{12 \div} =$ 　　　　　37. $\dfrac{25 \div}{40 \div} =$

38. $\dfrac{8 \div}{24 \div} =$ 　　　　　39. $\dfrac{6 \div}{54 \div} =$

40. $\dfrac{12 \div}{18 \div} =$ 　　　　　41. $\dfrac{20 \div}{30 \div} =$

Complete each fraction chain.

42. $\dfrac{16}{8} = \dfrac{}{4} = \dfrac{}{2}$ 　　　　43. $\dfrac{}{20} = \dfrac{}{10} = \dfrac{}{5}$

44. $\dfrac{}{12} = \dfrac{}{6} = \dfrac{}{3}$ 　　　　45. $\dfrac{}{8} = \dfrac{}{4} = \dfrac{}{2}$

▶ Find a Common Unit Fraction Using Fraction Bars

Read and discuss the Puzzled Penguin problem.

On Monday, Puzzled Penguin and his parents each ate $\frac{1}{3}$ of a fish. On Tuesday, they and Puzzled Penguin's friend each ate $\frac{1}{4}$ of a fish. Both fish were the same size. Puzzled Penguin wanted to know what fraction of a fish he ate on both Monday and Tuesday.

This is what Puzzled Penguin wrote: $\frac{1}{3} + \frac{1}{4} = \frac{2}{7}$

1. How did Puzzled Penguin add $\frac{1}{3}$ and $\frac{1}{4}$?

_____

2. Is Puzzled Penguin's addition correct? Use the fraction strips below if needed.

_____

Fish 1	$\frac{1}{3}$		$\frac{1}{3}$		$\frac{1}{3}$	
Fish 2	$\frac{1}{4}$	$\frac{1}{4}$		$\frac{1}{4}$		$\frac{1}{4}$
Total	$\frac{1}{7}$ $\frac{1}{7}$	$\frac{1}{7}$	$\frac{1}{7}$	$\frac{1}{7}$	$\frac{1}{7}$	$\frac{1}{7}$

Discuss how the twelfths fraction bar can help Puzzled Penguin with his addition.

	Fish 1 $\frac{1}{3}$						Fish 2 $\frac{1}{4}$					
Total	$\frac{1}{12}$	$\frac{1}{12}$	$\frac{1}{12}$	$\frac{1}{12}$	$\frac{1}{12}$	$\frac{1}{12}$	$\frac{1}{12}$	$\frac{1}{12}$	$\frac{1}{12}$	$\frac{1}{12}$	$\frac{1}{12}$	$\frac{1}{12}$

3. Use the fraction bars to rename $\frac{1}{3}$ and $\frac{1}{4}$ using the unit fraction $\frac{1}{12}$.

$\frac{1}{3} = \frac{}{12}$ and $\frac{1}{4} = \frac{}{12}$

4. Add the renamed fractions.

$\frac{1}{3} + \frac{1}{4} = \frac{}{12} + \frac{}{12} = \frac{+}{12} = \frac{}{12}$

Vocabulary

common denominator

▶ **Find a Common Unit Fraction Numerically**

5. Show how we could rename $\frac{1}{3}$ and $\frac{1}{4}$ numerically so that they have the same unit fraction.

$$\frac{1 \times}{3 \times} = \frac{}{12} \qquad \frac{1 \times}{4 \times} = \frac{}{12}$$

6. How is the denominator of the new unit fraction, $\frac{1}{12}$, related numerically to the denominators of $\frac{1}{3}$ and $\frac{1}{4}$?

▶ **Add Fractions With Unlike Denominators**

To add unlike fractions, you need to rewrite the fractions so they have a **common denominator**. A common denominator is a number that is a multiple of both denominators. For $\frac{1}{3}$ and $\frac{1}{4}$, 12 is a common denominator because it is a multiple of both 3 and 4.

7. Three runners are running in a relay race. The first runner goes $\frac{3}{10}$ of the total distance. The second runner goes $\frac{2}{5}$ of the total distance. Using the fraction bars or a numerical method, find the fraction of the distance the first two runners complete together.

$\frac{1}{5}$	$\frac{1}{5}$	$\frac{1}{5}$	$\frac{1}{5}$	$\frac{1}{5}$

$\frac{1}{10}$	$\frac{1}{10}$	$\frac{1}{10}$	$\frac{1}{10}$	$\frac{1}{10}$	$\frac{1}{10}$	$\frac{1}{10}$	$\frac{1}{10}$	$\frac{1}{10}$	$\frac{1}{10}$

$$\frac{2 \times}{5 \times} = \frac{}{10}$$

$$\frac{3}{10} + \frac{2}{5} = \frac{3}{10} + \frac{}{10} = \frac{+}{10} = \frac{}{10}$$

Class Activity

Name _____ Date _____

▶ Add Fractions With Unlike Denominators (continued)

In problem 7, you used 10 as the common denominator for $\frac{3}{10}$ and $\frac{2}{5}$. We say that 10 is the **least common denominator** of $\frac{3}{10}$ and $\frac{2}{5}$ because it is the smallest number that is a multiple of both 10 and 5. Using the least common denominator will give you fractions with smaller numbers that are easier to work with.

8. Lanny's parents brought two same-size cakes to the Parents' Club meeting at school. Lanny's mother served $\frac{3}{4}$ of her cake. Lanny's father served $\frac{5}{6}$ of his cake. Using the fraction bars or a numerical method, find the fraction of cake served in all.

$\frac{1}{4}$	$\frac{1}{4}$	$\frac{1}{4}$	$\frac{1}{4}$

$\frac{1}{12}$	$\frac{1}{12}$	$\frac{1}{12}$	$\frac{1}{12}$	$\frac{1}{12}$	$\frac{1}{12}$	$\frac{1}{12}$	$\frac{1}{12}$	$\frac{1}{12}$	$\frac{1}{12}$	$\frac{1}{12}$	$\frac{1}{12}$

$\frac{1}{6}$	$\frac{1}{6}$	$\frac{1}{6}$	$\frac{1}{6}$	$\frac{1}{6}$	$\frac{1}{6}$

$$\frac{3 \times}{4 \times} = \frac{}{12} \qquad \frac{5 \times}{6 \times} = \frac{}{12}$$

$$\frac{3}{4} + \frac{5}{6} = \frac{}{12} + \frac{}{12} = \frac{+}{12} = \frac{}{12}$$

9. Below are the additions you did in problems 4–8. Describe how the strategies you used to find fractions with like denominators in the following problems were alike and different.

$$\frac{1}{3} + \frac{1}{4} \qquad \frac{3}{10} + \frac{2}{5} \qquad \frac{3}{4} + \frac{5}{6}$$

_____

_____

_____

_____

Class Activity

▶ **Find Equivalent Fractions With Fraction Bars**

10. How do these fraction bars show equivalent fractions
for $\frac{1}{3}$?

_____

$\frac{1}{3}$	$\frac{1}{3}$	$\frac{1}{3}$
$\frac{1}{6}$ $\frac{1}{6}$	$\frac{1}{6}$ $\frac{1}{6}$	$\frac{1}{6}$ $\frac{1}{6}$
$\frac{1}{9}$ $\frac{1}{9}$ $\frac{1}{9}$	$\frac{1}{9}$ $\frac{1}{9}$ $\frac{1}{9}$	$\frac{1}{9}$ $\frac{1}{9}$ $\frac{1}{9}$
$\frac{1}{12}$ $\frac{1}{12}$ $\frac{1}{12}$ $\frac{1}{12}$	$\frac{1}{12}$ $\frac{1}{12}$ $\frac{1}{12}$ $\frac{1}{12}$	$\frac{1}{12}$ $\frac{1}{12}$ $\frac{1}{12}$ $\frac{1}{12}$
$\frac{1}{15}$ $\frac{1}{15}$ $\frac{1}{15}$ $\frac{1}{15}$ $\frac{1}{15}$	$\frac{1}{15}$ $\frac{1}{15}$ $\frac{1}{15}$ $\frac{1}{15}$ $\frac{1}{15}$	$\frac{1}{15}$ $\frac{1}{15}$ $\frac{1}{15}$ $\frac{1}{15}$ $\frac{1}{15}$
$\frac{1}{18}$ $\frac{1}{18}$ $\frac{1}{18}$ $\frac{1}{18}$ $\frac{1}{18}$ $\frac{1}{18}$	$\frac{1}{18}$ $\frac{1}{18}$ $\frac{1}{18}$ $\frac{1}{18}$ $\frac{1}{18}$ $\frac{1}{18}$	$\frac{1}{18}$ $\frac{1}{18}$ $\frac{1}{18}$ $\frac{1}{18}$ $\frac{1}{18}$ $\frac{1}{18}$

11. You can show how to find fractions equivalent to $\frac{1}{3}$
numerically. Fill in the blanks and finish the equations.
Then explain how these fraction equations show
equivalent fractions.

2 equal parts	3 equal parts	4 equal parts	__ equal parts	__ equal parts
× 2	× 3	× __	× __	× __
$\frac{1 \times 2}{3 \times 2} = \frac{2}{6}$	$\frac{1 \times}{3 \times} = \frac{}{9}$	$\frac{1 \times}{3 \times} = \frac{}{12}$	$\frac{1 \times}{3 \times} = \frac{}{15}$	$\frac{1 \times}{3 \times} = \frac{}{18}$

_____

_____

_____

_____

Class Activity

▶ Find Equivalent Fractions With the Multiplication Table

Multiplication table rows show relationships among equivalent fractions.

12. What happens to the fractions as you move from right to left? How does the size of the unit fraction change? How does the number of unit fractions change?

_____

_____

_____

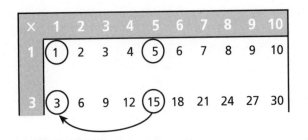

Simplify fractions.

13. What happens to the fractions as you move from left to right? How does the size of the unit fraction change? How does the number of unit fractions change?

_____

_____

×	1	2	3	4	5	6	7	8	9	10
1	1	2	3	4	5	6	7	8	9	10
3	3	6	9	12	15	18	21	24	27	30

Unsimplify fractions to get a common denominator to add, subtract, or compare them.

Name _____ **Date** _____

▶ Discuss and Add Unlike Fractions

Find a common denominator. Then add.

	Find the common denominator.	**Add the fractions.**

14. $\dfrac{1}{4} + \dfrac{3}{8}$ $\dfrac{1 \times 2}{4 \times 2} = \dfrac{2}{\square}$ $\dfrac{3}{8}$ $\dfrac{2}{\square} + \dfrac{3}{\square} = \dfrac{2 + 3}{\square} = \dfrac{5}{\square}$

15. $\dfrac{1}{6} + \dfrac{3}{8}$ $\dfrac{1 \times 4}{6 \times 4} = \dfrac{4}{\square}$ $\dfrac{3 \times 3}{8 \times 3} = \dfrac{9}{\square}$ $\dfrac{4}{\square} + \dfrac{9}{\square} = \dfrac{4 + 9}{\square} = \dfrac{13}{\square}$

16. $\dfrac{2}{5} + \dfrac{3}{8}$

17. $\dfrac{1}{4} + \dfrac{7}{10}$

18. $\dfrac{5}{12} + \dfrac{2}{3}$

19. $\dfrac{5}{6} + \dfrac{3}{4}$

20. $\dfrac{4}{7} + \dfrac{5}{6}$

21. $\dfrac{2}{5} + \dfrac{4}{10}$

22. $\dfrac{3}{7} + \dfrac{2}{14}$

23. $\dfrac{1}{4} + \dfrac{5}{12}$

Add Fractions With Unlike Denominators

Name _____

Date _____

Class Activity

▶ Find Equivalent Fractions

On Monday, Puzzled Penguin and his parents each ate $\frac{1}{3}$ of a fish. On Tuesday, they and Puzzled Penguin's friend each ate $\frac{1}{4}$ of a fish. Both fish were the same size. Puzzled Penguin wanted to know which day he ate more fish. He also wanted to know how much more fish he ate on that day.

1. Use fraction bars to answer Puzzled Penguin's questions. Which day did he eat more fish? How much more?

_____

2. Complete the numeric solution under the fraction bars. What number goes in the ⬚ boxes?

_____

Monday	$\frac{1}{3}$	$\frac{1}{3}$	$\frac{1}{3}$

Tuesday	$\frac{1}{4}$	$\frac{1}{4}$	$\frac{1}{4}$	$\frac{1}{4}$

Total	$\frac{1}{12}$	$\frac{1}{12}$	$\frac{1}{12}$	$\frac{1}{12}$	$\frac{1}{12}$	$\frac{1}{12}$	$\frac{1}{12}$	$\frac{1}{12}$	$\frac{1}{12}$	$\frac{1}{12}$	$\frac{1}{12}$	$\frac{1}{12}$

Find equivalent fractions.

$\frac{1 \times 4}{3 \times 4} = \frac{4}{\square}$ $\frac{1 \times 3}{4 \times 3} = \frac{3}{\square}$

Compare.

$\frac{1}{3} \bigcirc \frac{1}{4}$ $\frac{4}{12} \bigcirc \frac{3}{12}$

Subtract.

$\frac{4}{12} - \frac{3}{12} = \frac{4-3}{12} = \frac{1}{12}$

3. Here is how Puzzled Penguin solved his problem. What mistakes did he make? Why is his solution wrong?

$\frac{1}{4} - \frac{1}{3} = \frac{0}{1} = 0$

_____

_____

▶ Compare Fractions

Show your work.

4. Sue ate $\frac{3}{8}$ of a melon. Ron ate $\frac{2}{5}$ of a melon that was the same size. Who ate more?

_____

Compare and Subtract Fractions With Unlike Denominators **383**

▶ Solve Problems With Unlike Fractions

Solve.

Show your work.

5. On Monday, Roberto read $\frac{1}{5}$ of a novel. On Tuesday, he read $\frac{3}{7}$ of the novel. How much of the novel did he read in the two days?

_____

6. Alyssa ate $\frac{3}{5}$ of a box of raisins, and Lou ate $\frac{1}{6}$ of the box. What fraction of the box was left?

_____

7. Paul jogged for $\frac{2}{10}$ of an hour. Inez jogged for $\frac{5}{8}$ of an hour. Who jogged for a longer period of time? How much longer?

_____

For each pair of fractions, find equivalent fractions with a common denominator. Then compare, add, and subtract.

Fractions	Equivalent Fractions	Compare.
8. $\frac{2}{3}$ $\frac{4}{5}$	$\frac{2 \times}{3 \times} = \boxed{}$ $\frac{4 \times}{5 \times} = \boxed{}$	$\frac{2}{3} \bigcirc \frac{4}{5}$

Add.

$\boxed{} + \boxed{} = \frac{\boxed{} + \boxed{}}{\boxed{}} = \boxed{}$

Subtract.

$\boxed{} - \boxed{} = \frac{\boxed{} - \boxed{}}{\boxed{}} = \boxed{}$

Fractions	Equivalent Fractions	Compare.
9. $\frac{3}{4}$ $\frac{2}{5}$	$\frac{3 \times}{4 \times} = \boxed{}$ $\frac{2 \times}{5 \times} = \boxed{}$	$\frac{3}{4} \bigcirc \frac{2}{5}$

Add.

$\boxed{} + \boxed{} = \frac{\boxed{} + \boxed{}}{\boxed{}} = \boxed{}$

Subtract.

$\boxed{} - \boxed{} = \frac{\boxed{} - \boxed{}}{\boxed{}} = \boxed{}$

Order the fractions from greatest to least.

10. $\frac{1}{2}, \frac{1}{4}, \frac{3}{8}$ _____

11. $\frac{2}{3}, \frac{5}{6}, \frac{4}{9}$ _____

Compare and Subtract Fractions With Unlike Denominators

► Compare, Add, and Subtract Fractions

For each pair of fractions, find an equivalent fraction. Then compare the fractions, add them, and subtract the smaller fraction from the larger one. An example is shown below for $\frac{1}{2}$ and $\frac{5}{7}$.

Find equivalent fractions.	Compare.	Add.	Subtract.
$\frac{1}{2} = \frac{7}{14}$ $\quad$ $\frac{5}{7} = \frac{10}{14}$	$\frac{1}{2} < \frac{5}{7}$	$\frac{1}{2} + \frac{5}{7} = \frac{17}{14}$	$\frac{5}{7} - \frac{1}{2} = \frac{3}{14}$

1. $\frac{5}{6}, \frac{2}{3}$

2. $\frac{1}{4}, \frac{3}{8}$

3. $\frac{1}{2}, \frac{5}{8}$

4. $\frac{11}{12}, \frac{5}{6}$

5. $\frac{2}{5}, \frac{3}{10}$

6. $\frac{3}{5}, \frac{5}{7}$

7. $\frac{3}{4}, \frac{2}{3}$

8. $\frac{2}{3}, \frac{9}{12}$

9. $\frac{5}{8}, \frac{4}{7}$

► Solve Problems With Fractions

Solve each problem.

Show your work.

10. At Kim's family reunion, a large cake was served for dessert. The children ate $\frac{2}{3}$ of the cake. The adults ate $\frac{1}{4}$ of the cake. Did the family eat all of the cake? Explain your thinking.

11. Maria's grandmother lives $\frac{5}{8}$ of the distance from Maria's home to Maria's school. Maria's uncle lives $\frac{7}{12}$ of the distance from Maria's home to her school. Who lives closer to Maria? How much closer?

12. Greta has a bag of 60 green and blue marbles. One at a time, she pulls out 6 marbles, returning each marble to the bag when she pulls it out. She gets 2 green marbles and 4 blue marbles. She says, "Now I know my bag contains 20 green and 40 blue marbles." Is she right or wrong? Explain your thinking.

13. Jerome and Sherry are playing a game. They roll a number cube to see who goes first. Jerome rolls a 6. Sherry also rolls a 6. Jerome thinks Sherry cheated because a 6 should come up only 1 out of 6 times. Is he right or wrong? Explain your thinking.

Class Activity

Name _____ **Date** _____

► Coin Toss Experiment

When you toss a coin, heads and tails are **equally likely** results. This means they have the same chance of occurring.

A **probability** is a number between 0 and 1 that tells you how likely something is to happen. When you toss a coin, you can expect to get heads about half the time, or on about 1 out of every 2 tosses. The probability of getting heads is $\frac{1}{2}$.

1. Toss a coin ten times and keep a tally.

Heads	Tails

Did you get heads for half of your tosses? _____

2. Find the total number of heads and the total number of tails tossed by everyone in your group.

Group results: _____ Heads   _____ Tails

Did your group get heads on half of its tosses? _____

3. Work with your teacher to combine the results for everyone in your class.

Class results: _____ Heads   _____ Tails

Did your class get heads on half of its tosses? _____

4. If the probability of getting heads is $\frac{1}{2}$, why didn't everyone get heads on half their tosses?

_____

_____

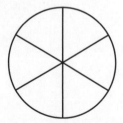

Name _____

Date _____

Class Activity

▶ Solve Probability Problems

5. Misha puts 15 glass marbles and 10 metal marbles in a bag. If she pulls 1 marble without looking, what is the probability it will be metal? _____

6. Three of Misha's glass marbles are green. If she puts all 15 glass marbles in a bag and picks one, what is the probability she will get a green marble? _____

7. Of the 10 metal marbles, 7 are brass and 3 are steel. If Misha puts the metal marbles in the bag and chooses one, what is the probability it will be brass? _____

▶ Analyze a Spinner

Suppose you spin this spinner once. Solve each problem.

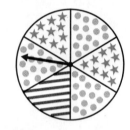

8. What is the probability the arrow will land in a space with dots?

   _____

9. What is the probability the spinner will land in a space with stars?

   _____

10. What is the probability the spinner will land in a space with stripes?

   _____

11. Use one of the divided circles below to design your own spinner. Ask your partner probability questions about your spinner.

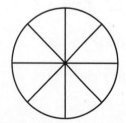
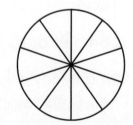

Vocabulary

frequency table
line plot

► Make a Line Plot

A number of students each tossed a number cube once. How often each number was rolled is shown in the **frequency table** below.

Outcome	Number of Students
1	6
2	3
3	5
4	4
5	2
6	5

We can use a line plot to show the frequency of the data. A **line plot** is a graphic way to compare the data.

1. Make a line plot of the data.

2. How many students altogether tossed a cube? Explain how you know.

_____

_____

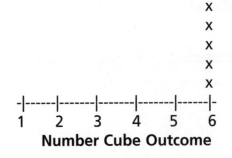

Number Cube Outcome

3. Describe the shape of the data.

_____

_____

_____

4. Suppose the experiment was repeated. Would you expect the line plot of the results to look exactly the same as the line plot above? Explain why or why not.

_____

_____

_____

► Analyze a Line Plot

Serena would like to spend as much time as possible babysitting during the summer, but she does not know what amount of money to charge per hour. So she asked other students in her school what they charge. The amounts they named are shown in the line plot below.

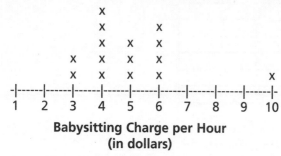

Babysitting Charge per Hour
(in dollars)

► Statistics and Line Plots

Solve.

5. If Serena chooses to charge an amount that is equal to the median of the data, what amount would she charge?

_____

6. If Serena chooses to charge an amount that is equal to the mode of the data, what amount would she charge?

_____

7. If Serena chooses to charge an amount that is equal to the range of the data, what amount would she charge?

_____

8. What amount per hour do you think Serena should charge? Explain why.

_____

_____

_____

Display and Analyze Data

Name _____ **Date** _____

Class Activity

▶ A Whole Number Times a Unit Fraction

The lunchroom at Mandy's school serves pizza every Friday. Each slice is $\frac{1}{4}$ of a pizza. Mandy eats one slice every week.

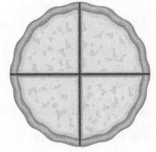

Solve each problem, first by adding and then by multiplying. Show your work.

1. What fraction of a pizza does Mandy eat in 3 weeks?

_____

2. What fraction of a pizza does Mandy eat in 5 weeks?

_____

3. What fraction of a pizza does Mandy eat in 11 weeks?

_____

▶ Practice and Generalize

Draw, shade, and label shapes to show the solution to each problem. You can use long bars if you want.

4. $2 \times \frac{1}{3}$

5. $6 \times \frac{1}{5}$

6. $10 \times \frac{1}{8}$

7. $3 \times \frac{1}{4}$

8. $8 \times \frac{1}{3}$

9. $14 \times \frac{1}{7}$

Class Activity

Name _____

Date _____

▶ A Whole Number Times a Non-Unit Fraction

At Joe's school, the lunchroom serves sub sandwiches every Thursday. Each piece is $\frac{1}{6}$ of a whole sub. Joe eats 2 pieces every Thursday.

Solve each problem, first by adding and then by multiplying.

Show your work.

10. How much of a sub sandwich does Joe eat every Thursday?

_____

11. What fraction of a sub does Joe eat in 3 weeks?

_____

12. What fraction of a sub does Joe eat in 5 weeks?

_____

▶ Practice and Generalize

Solve.

13. $8 \times \frac{3}{4} =$

14. $18 \times \frac{2}{3} =$

15. $10 \times \frac{5}{6} =$

16. $4 \times \frac{5}{7} =$

17. $4 \times \frac{3}{8} =$

18. $15 \times \frac{3}{10} =$

19. $3 \times \frac{4}{5} =$

20. $7 \times \frac{8}{9} =$

Multiply a Fraction by a Whole Number

Class Activity

▶ A Unit Fraction of a Whole Number

The librarian put 30 books on the shelves in 6 equal piles.

1. What fraction of the 30 books does each pile show? _____

2. Write a division equation that shows the number of books in each pile. _____

3. You can also write a multiplication equation to show the number of books in each pile. Discuss the equations below.

of means *times*	*of* means *times*
6 groups *of* 5 = 30	a $\frac{1}{6}$ group *of* 30 = 5
6 × 5 = 30	$\frac{1}{6}$ × 30 = 5

4. Discuss the relationship between division by a whole number and multiplication by a unit fraction.

   30 books ÷ 6 equal piles = 5 books per pile   30 ÷ 6 = 5

   $\frac{1}{6}$ of 30 books = $\frac{1}{6}$ of 30 = 5 books $\frac{1}{6}$ × 30 = 5

Find the unit fraction $\frac{1}{d}$ of each whole number by making *d* equal shares.

Examples: $\frac{1}{3} \times 15 = 15 \div 3 = \frac{15}{3} = 5$ $\frac{1}{4} \times 28 = 28 \div 4 = \frac{28}{4} = 7$

5. $\frac{1}{7} \times 14 =$ _____   6. $\frac{1}{8} \times 40 =$ _____

7. $\frac{1}{3} \times 12 =$ _____   8. $\frac{1}{6} \times 60 =$ _____

9. $\frac{1}{9} \times 63 =$ _____   10. $\frac{1}{3} \times 27 =$ _____

11. $\frac{1}{4} \times 10 =$ _____   12. $\frac{1}{5} \times 19 =$ _____

▶ A Fraction of a Whole Number

Jim, Tina, and Maurice shelved the piles of library books. Sketch the books below.

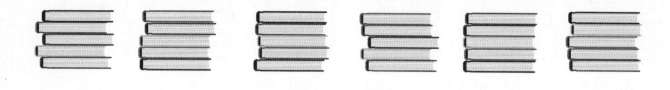

_____   _____   _____   _____   _____   _____

Jim reshelved 1 of the piles.

13. What fraction of the books did Jim shelve? _____

14. How many books did he shelve? _____

15. Circle the books Jim shelved and write his name under them.

Tina reshelved 2 of the piles.

16. What fraction of the books did Tina shelve? _____

17. How many books did she shelve? _____

18. How many times as many books did Tina shelve
    as Jim? _____

19. Circle the books Tina shelved and write her name under them.

Maurice reshelved 3 of the piles.

20. What fraction of the books did Maurice shelve? _____

21. How many books did he shelve? _____

22. How many times as many books did Maurice shelve
    as Jim? _____

23. Circle the books Maurice shelved and write his name under them.

24. Have the three students shelved all the books? How do you know?

_____

▶ Any Fraction of a Whole Number

Find the fraction of each whole number. Use 5 to 12 if they help.

| **Examples:** $\frac{2}{3} \times 15 = 2 \times (\frac{1}{3} \times 15) = 2 \times (\frac{15}{3}) = 2 \times 5 = 10$ |

25. $\frac{2}{7} \times 14 =$ _____

26. $\frac{7}{8} \times 40 =$ _____

27. $\frac{2}{3} \times 12 =$ _____

28. $\frac{3}{6} \times 60 =$ _____

29. $\frac{4}{9} \times 63 =$ _____

30. $\frac{2}{3} \times 27 =$ _____

31. $\frac{3}{4} \times 10 =$ _____

32. $\frac{2}{5} \times 19 =$ _____

▶ Solve Word Problems

Show your work.

33. Carlo saw 35 fish at the aquarium. $\frac{1}{5}$ of them were clownfish. How many fish were clownfish?

_____

34. Gayle has 36 marbles. $\frac{2}{6}$ of the marbles are green. How many marbles are green?

_____

35. Hayden is stacking 24 books into piles. He is putting $\frac{2}{8}$ of the books into each pile. How many books are in each pile?

_____

36. Sarah had 54 carrot sticks. She put $\frac{2}{9}$ of the carrot sticks onto each plate. How many carrot sticks are on each plate?

_____

37. **On the Back** Explain in your own words how to find a fraction of a whole number. Give an example.

▶ Compare Lengths

Asha made a long thin snake out of clay. Her little brother
Sam made a short fat snake.

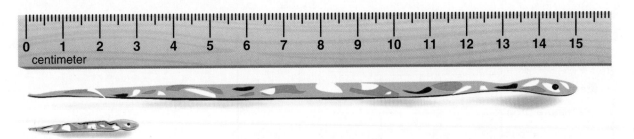

**Complete these addition comparison statements. In the second
blank, insert the word *shorter* or *longer*.**

1. Asha's snake is _____ cm _____ than Sam's snake.

2. Sam's snake is _____ cm _____ than Asha's snake.

**Now complete these statements to compare the snakes
with multiplication.**

3. Asha's snake is _____ as long as Sam's snake.

4. Sam's snake is _____ as long as Asha's snake.

5. Draw comparison bars to show the multiplication
   comparisons.

▶ Bar Graphs

The bar graph below shows how many people went on the seven most popular rides at an amusement park.

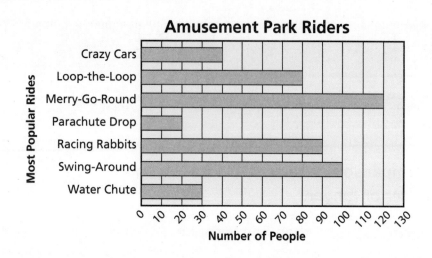

Amusement Park Riders

Most Popular Rides: Crazy Cars, Loop-the-Loop, Merry-Go-Round, Parachute Drop, Racing Rabbits, Swing-Around, Water Chute

Number of People

6. Find two pairs of values on the graph that are exact multiples of each other. For each pair, draw and label comparison bars and write two equations (with letters) to show the comparison. An example is shown below:

Loop-the-Loop (*l*) | 40 | 40 | $l = 2 \times c$ $80 = 2 \times 40$

Crazy Cars (*c*) | 40 | $c = \frac{1}{2} \times l$ $40 = \frac{1}{2} \times 80$

Fraction Comparisons

▶ Discuss Leading and Misleading Language

To solve comparison word problems, first decide which is the large amount and which is the small amount.

There are 7 fiddle players at the country music festival.
There are $\frac{1}{5}$ as many fiddle players as guitar players.
How many guitar players are there?

7. Draw comparison bars to see the problem. Then write the other multiplication comparison sentence.

There are _____ guitar players.

_____

_____

_____

8. Solve the problems on page 400. Then write your own multiplication comparison word problem with misleading language.

_____

_____

_____

_____

_____

▶ Other Comparison Problems

Solve. Draw comparison bars if you need to. Then write the other multiplication comparison sentence.

Show your work.

9. Frank made 10 goals at the hockey game. He made 5 times as many goals as Josie made. How many goals did Josie make?

   Josie made _____ goals.

   _____

   _____

10. Su-Lin has $15. Zane has $\frac{1}{3}$ as much money as Su-Lin. How much money does Zane have?

    Zane has _____.

    _____

    _____

11. On a cattle ranch, 32 calves were born this year. That was 4 times as many calves as were born last year. How many calves were born last year?

    _____ calves were born last year.

    _____

    _____

    _____

12. Ella practiced piano 3 hours this week. She spent $\frac{1}{6}$ as much time practicing as Ramón did. How many hours did Ramón practice?

    Ramón practiced _____ hours this week.

    _____

    _____

▶ Discuss Number Lines

The number line below shows the fourths between 0 and 1. Discuss how the number line is like and unlike the fraction bar above it.

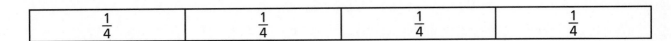

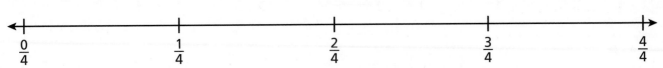

These number lines are divided to show different fractions.

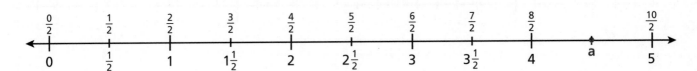

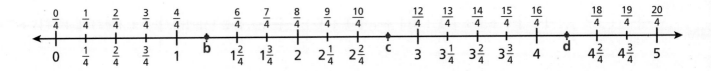

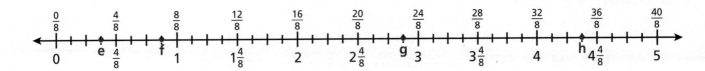

Complete the equivalent fraction equations.

1. $\dfrac{1}{2} = \dfrac{}{4}$

2. $\dfrac{1}{4} = \dfrac{}{8}$

3. $\dfrac{6}{8} = \dfrac{}{4}$

4. $\dfrac{2}{4} = \dfrac{}{8}$

▶ Identify Points

5. Write the fraction or mixed number for each lettered point above.

a. _____   b. _____   c. _____   d. _____

e. _____   f. _____   g. _____   h. _____

▶ **Number Lines for Thirds, Sixths, and Ninths**

Tell how many equal parts are between zero and 1.
Then write fraction labels above the equal parts.

6. _____

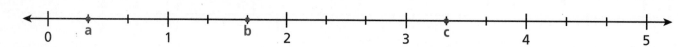

7. _____

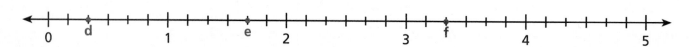

8. _____

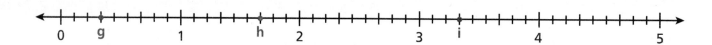

▶ **Identify Points**

9. Write the fraction or mixed number for each lettered
point above. Describe any patterns you see with the class.

a. _____   b. _____   c. _____

d. _____   e. _____   f. _____

g. _____   h. _____   i. _____

For each fraction or mixed number, label that point
on the number line with its letter.

10.

a. $\frac{1}{5}$ b. $\frac{7}{10}$ c. $1\frac{2}{5}$ d. $2\frac{1}{2}$

e. $3\frac{3}{10}$ f. $4\frac{2}{5}$ g. $4\frac{9}{10}$ h. $5\frac{1}{2}$

Fractions on the Number Line

▶ Compare and Order Fractions

Write >, <, or = to make each statement true.

1. $\frac{3}{8}$ ◯ $\frac{1}{4}$ 2. $\frac{4}{9}$ ◯ $\frac{1}{2}$ 3. $\frac{2}{6}$ ◯ $\frac{3}{9}$ 4. $\frac{5}{6}$ ◯ $\frac{11}{12}$

5. $\frac{1}{4}$ ◯ $\frac{1}{6}$ 6. $\frac{3}{7}$ ◯ $\frac{3}{5}$ 7. $\frac{1}{9}$ ◯ $\frac{1}{8}$ 8. $\frac{6}{7}$ ◯ $\frac{6}{8}$

Write the fractions in order from greatest to least.

9. $\frac{1}{7}, \frac{1}{2}, \frac{1}{5}$ _____

10. $\frac{3}{8}, \frac{3}{6}, \frac{3}{10}$ _____

11. $\frac{5}{9}, \frac{5}{6}, \frac{5}{7}$ _____

12. $\frac{5}{3}, \frac{5}{12}, \frac{5}{6}$ _____

13. $\frac{1}{10}, \frac{1}{5}, \frac{1}{20}$ _____

14. $\frac{3}{8}, \frac{3}{2}, \frac{3}{4}$ _____

▶ Add and Subtract Fractions

Add each pair of fractions. Then subtract the smaller fraction from the larger fraction.

15. $\frac{4}{7}, \frac{2}{7}$

16. $\frac{2}{6}, \frac{3}{6}$

17. $\frac{2}{3}, \frac{4}{5}$

18. $\frac{3}{8}, \frac{3}{4}$

19. $5\frac{1}{3}, 2\frac{5}{6}$

20. $4\frac{3}{5}, 9\frac{1}{2}$

▶ Simplify Fractions

Write the simplest equivalent fraction.

21. $\frac{21}{28} = $ _____

22. $\frac{12}{36} = $ _____

23. $\frac{42}{48} = $ _____

24. $\frac{10}{45} = $ _____

25. $\frac{8}{18} = $ _____

26. $\frac{24}{30} = $ _____

Class Activity

Name _____ **Date** _____

► Multiply Fractions and Whole Numbers

Multiply.

27. $\frac{1}{7} \times 21 =$ _____

28. $25 \times \frac{3}{5} =$ _____

29. $56 \times \frac{3}{8} =$ _____

30. $\frac{1}{4} \times 36 =$ _____

31. $36 \times \frac{5}{9} =$ _____

32. $\frac{2}{3} \times 27 =$ _____

Solve each problem.

Show your work.

33. Mario has 18 pencils. He sharpens $\frac{1}{6}$ of them before class. How many does he sharpen?

_____

34. Jason had 45 marbles. He gave $\frac{1}{5}$ of them to a friend. How many did he give away? How many does he have left?

_____

_____

35. Janie's book is 124 pages long. She is on page 63. Is she more or less than halfway finished with her book? Tell how you know.

_____

_____

36. Michelle has 4 textbooks. Each weighs $\frac{5}{8}$ pound. What is the total weight of her textbooks?

_____

37. Label the point for each fraction or mixed number with the corresponding letter.

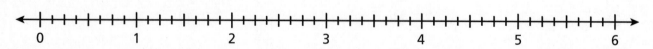

a. $\frac{3}{8}$ b. $\frac{3}{4}$ c. $1\frac{1}{2}$ d. $2\frac{1}{8}$ e. $2\frac{7}{8}$

f. $3\frac{1}{4}$ g. $3\frac{5}{8}$ h. $4\frac{2}{4}$ i. $4\frac{6}{8}$ j. $5\frac{1}{4}$

Practice With Fractions

▶ Math and Art

The designs below are called tessellations. A **tessellation** is a repeating pattern that covers a surface with no overlaps or gaps.

   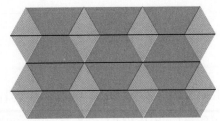

A designer at Tim's Tabletop Company is making some patterns for tables with tile tops. You can help the designer. Use pattern blocks and Pattern Block Grid Paper to make some designs that are tessellations.

1. Make a tessellating design using one pattern block shape. Record your design on Pattern Block Grid Paper. What shape did you use?

   _____

2. Make a tessellating design using two Pattern Block shapes. Record your design on Pattern Block Grid Paper. What shapes did you use?

   _____

3. Make a tessellating design using three Pattern Block shapes. Record your design on Pattern Block Grid Paper. What shapes did you use?

   _____

4. Can you use make a tessellation with a circle? Why or why not?

   _____

Class Activity

▶ Data Collection Methods

5. You want to find which type of bread a group of people like the best—rye, white, or whole wheat. First you must decide what question to ask. Write your question.

_____

_____

6. Next you need to decide who you will survey. What will be the range of their ages? Will you ask males only, females only, or both?

_____

_____

7. Conduct the survey. Copy the chart below and record your results.

Type of Bread	Number of People
Rye	
White	
Whole Wheat	

8. Show the results of the survey in a bar graph. Use grid paper to make the graph.

9. Write a paragraph about how you collected the data. What did you do to make sure your survey was accurate?

_____

_____

_____

Use Mathematical Processes

Name _____ **Date** _____

Simplify each fraction.

1. $\dfrac{8 \div}{28 \div} =$

2. $\dfrac{24 \div}{40 \div} =$

3. Write 5 fractions equivalent to $\dfrac{1}{3}$.

_____ _____ _____ _____ _____

Write < or > to make a true statement.

4. $\dfrac{3}{7} \bigcirc \dfrac{3}{5}$

5. $\dfrac{2}{5} \bigcirc \dfrac{1}{2}$

6. $\dfrac{3}{4} \bigcirc \dfrac{2}{3}$

7. Label the point for each fraction or mixed number with the corresponding letter.

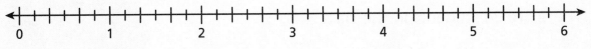

0   1   2   3   4   5   6

a. $1\dfrac{2}{3}$ b. $5\dfrac{1}{6}$ c. $\dfrac{1}{2}$ d. $3\dfrac{2}{6}$ e. $4\dfrac{1}{3}$

Add or subtract.

8. $\dfrac{5}{6} - \dfrac{1}{4} =$

9. $\dfrac{1}{8} + \dfrac{3}{4} =$

10. $3\dfrac{1}{2} - \dfrac{3}{4} =$

11. $4\dfrac{3}{5} + 2\dfrac{4}{5} =$

Multiply.

12. $4 \times \dfrac{1}{5} =$ _____

13. $\dfrac{3}{8} \times 24 =$ _____

14. a. A group of students each rolled a number cube one time. The frequency table shows the results. Use a line plot to show the frequency of the data. Give your plot a title.

Number Rolled	1	2	3	4	5	6
Frequency	6	3	6	2	4	4

b. Write a conclusion based on the data.

_____

15. Sketch a circle. Draw and label a radius on it.

Name _____ **Date** _____

Show your work

Solve.

16. Ryan studied math for 2 hours last weekend. He spent $\frac{1}{4}$ as much time studying as Clair. How much time did Clair spend studying math?

_____

17. Tara earns $6 per hour. Dawn earns $\frac{1}{3}$ as much. How much does Dawn earn per hour?

_____

Use the circle graph or the spinner to answer these questions. Show your work.

18. There are 24 students in the class.

   a. How many students prefer:

   cats _____   dogs _____

   b. Write a number sentence that shows what fraction of the class prefers fish and birds.

   _____

Class Pet Preferences

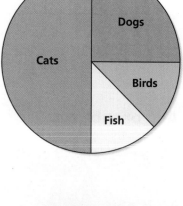

19. Suppose you spin this spinner once. What is the probability that it will land on a C?

   _____

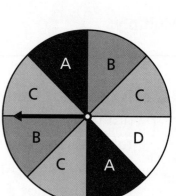

20. **Extended Response** Sketch a different spinner with 6 equal sections. Label it so the spinner is *most likely* to land on A. Explain why your spinner is most likely to land on A.

   _____

Class Activity

Name _____ Date _____

Vocabulary

circle
sphere
radius

▶ Spheres and Circles

Circles are flat and have two dimensions. **Spheres** are round solids and have three dimensions.

Write *circle* **or** *sphere* **for each picture.**

1.

_____

2.

_____

3.

_____

4.

_____

5.

_____

6.

_____

7. How are circles and spheres alike? How are they different?

_____

_____

_____

8. What is the **radius** of a circle? What is the radius of a sphere?

_____

_____

_____

Copyright © Houghton Mifflin Company. All rights reserved.

Vocabulary	
cube	surface area
face	net

► Cubes

A **cube** is a solid made of congruent **faces** that are square.

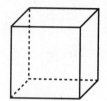

9. How many faces does a cube have? _____

10. Name a real-world object that is shaped like a cube.

_____

_____

11. Each edge of a cube measures 3 cm. What is the total
area of all of the faces? _____

12. Why is the total area of its faces called the
surface area of the cube?

_____

A **net** is a flat or plane figure that can be folded to form a
solid. The net at the right can be folded to form a cube.

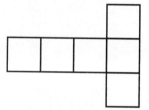

13. On a separate sheet of paper, draw several different
nets for a cube.

► Make Stacks of Cubes

How many cubes can you see?
How many cubes can you *not* see?
How many cubes are in each stack?

14. 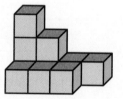   15.   16.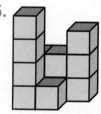

Cubes you can see: _____   _____   _____

Cubes you cannot see: _____   _____   _____

Total number of cubes: _____   _____   _____

Dear Family,

This unit is about solid figures, such as cubes, spheres, prisms, and cylinders.

During this unit, your child will learn how to recognize and name solid figures, and how to describe their characteristics. Your child will be working with the figures shown below.

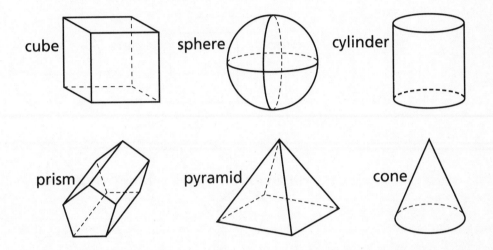

cube   sphere   cylinder

prism   pyramid   cone

The next unit involves fractions. As students work with fractions, they will need to multiply and divide. If your child needs practice with multiplication and division, you can help by providing him or her with as many opportunities as possible to do so. If you need practice materials or if you have any questions, please call or write to me.

Sincerely,
Your child's teacher

Estimada familia:

Esta unidad trata figuras geométricas, como cubos, esferas, prismas y cilindros.

Al estudiar esta unidad su niño aprenderá a reconocer y nombrar figuras geométricas y a describir sus características. Su niño trabajará con las figuras que se muestran a continuación.

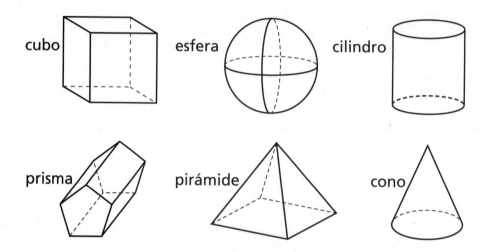

cubo esfera cilindro

prisma pirámide cono

La siguiente unidad trata las fracciones. Cuando los estudiantes trabajen con fracciones, tendrán que multiplicar y dividir. Si a su niño le hace falta practicar la multiplicación y la división, usted puede ayudarlo ofreciéndole todas las oportunidades de practicar que pueda. Si necesita materiales de práctica o si tiene preguntas, por favor comuníquese conmigo.

Atentamente,
El maestro de su niño

Spheres and Cubes

Vocabulary

prism
base
triangular prism

▶ Make a Prism

A **prism** is a solid figure with two congruent opposite faces called **bases**. Follow the steps below to make a **triangular prism**. The bases of your prism will be equilateral triangles whose sides measure 8 cm.

1. Measure and cut out two congruent bases for your triangular prism.

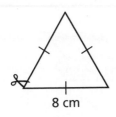
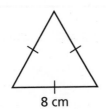

2. Calculate the perimeter of one base.

$$8 + 8 + 8 = 24 \text{ cm}$$
$$3 \times 8 = 24 \text{ cm}$$

3. Cut a sheet of paper so that its length is the same as the perimeter of a base.

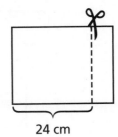

24 cm

4. Cut the paper to a height of your choice. This picture shows a height of 16 cm.

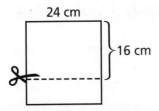

24 cm

16 cm

Hint: Don't cut your height too short.

5. Mark lines on the paper that divide the length into three equal parts.

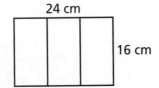

24 cm

16 cm

For a length of 24 cm, draw lines at 8 cm and 16 cm.

6. Fold along the lines and tape together the edges to make a prism.

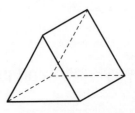

triangular prism

Class Activity

Vocabulary

cylinder

▶ Name Prisms

Name the shape of the base and use it to name the prism.

7.

_____

_____

8.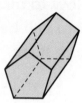

_____

_____

9.

_____

_____

10.

_____

_____

11.

_____

_____

12.

_____

_____

▶ Recognize Cylinders

A **cylinder** is another type of solid figure.

13. List some examples of real-world cylinders.

_____

_____

14. How are cylinders and prisms alike?

_____

_____

15. How are cylinders and prisms different?

_____

_____

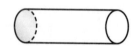

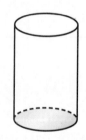

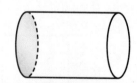

Prisms and Cylinders

Name

Date

▶ Find Surface Area

Name each prism. Write the area of each face on the net.
Add the areas to find the surface area of each prism.

16.

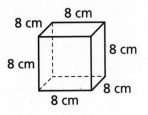

8 cm
8 cm
8 cm
8 cm
8 cm
8 cm

8 cm
8 cm
8 cm
8 cm
8 cm
8 cm
8 cm
8 cm

_____

_____

17.

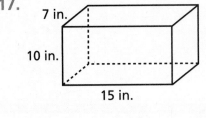

7 in.
10 in.
15 in.

7 in.
10 in.
7 in.
7 in.
15 in.
7 in.
15 in.

_____

_____

18.

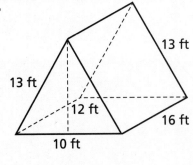

13 ft
13 ft
12 ft
16 ft
10 ft

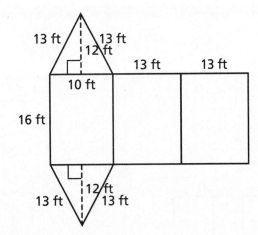

13 ft
13 ft
12 ft
10 ft
13 ft
13 ft
16 ft
12 ft
13 ft
13 ft

_____

_____

19. How can you find the surface area of any prism?

_____

_____

Going Further

► Match Nets and Solids

Match each net to a solid.

1.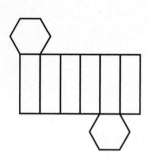

A

2.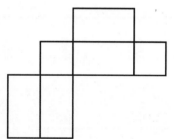

B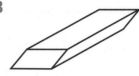

3.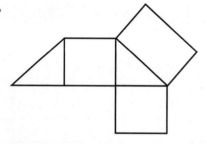

C

4.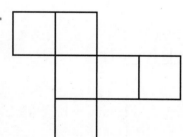

D

5.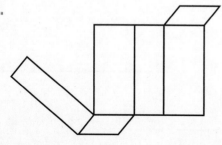

E

Prisms and Cylinders

Name _____ **Date** _____

▶ Discuss Solid Figures

Name each solid.

1.

_____

2.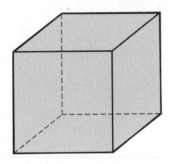

_____

3.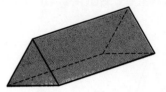

_____

4.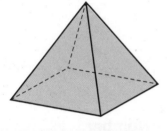

_____

5.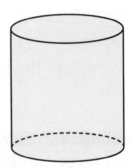

_____

6.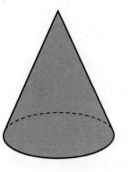

_____

▶ Discuss Faces, Edges, and Vertices

Write the number of faces, edges, and vertices for each solid.

7.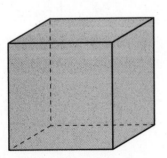

_____
_____
_____

8.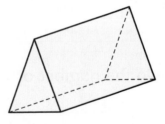

_____
_____
_____

9.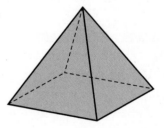

_____
_____
_____

► Faces, Edges, and Vertices of Prisms

A decagon has 10 sides. You can use patterns to predict the number of faces, edges, and vertices of a prism with a decagon as a base.

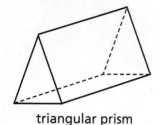

triangular prism

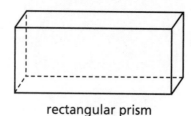

rectangular prism

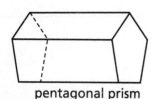

pentagonal prism

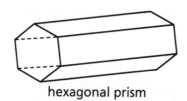

hexagonal prism

10. Use the prisms you see above to complete the next three rows of the chart.

Type of Prism	Number of Sides on Base	Number of Faces	Number of Edges	Number of Vertices
Triangular	3	5	9	6
Rectangular				
Pentagonal				
Hexagonal				
Decagonal				

11. What pattern do you notice in the number of faces?

_____

12. What pattern do you notice in the number of edges?

_____

13. What pattern do you notice in the number of vertices?

_____

14. Use the patterns you noticed to complete the last row of the chart.

Compare and Contrast Solids

▶ Faces, Edges, and Vertices of Pyramids

An octagon has eight sides. You can use patterns to predict the number of faces, edges, and vertices of a pyramid with an octagon as a base.

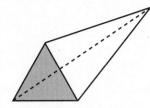

triangular pyramid

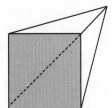

square pyramid

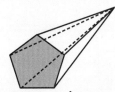

pentagonal pyramid

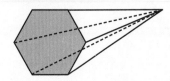

hexagonal pyramid

15. Use the prisms you see above to complete the next three rows of the chart.

Type of Pyramid	Number of Sides on Base	Number of Faces	Number of Edges	Number of Vertices
Triangular	3	4	6	4
Square				
Pentagonal				
Hexagonal				
Octagonal				

16. What pattern do you notice in the number of faces?

_____

17. What pattern do you notice in the number of edges?

_____

18. What pattern do you notice in the number of vertices?

_____

19. Use the pattern you notice to complete the last row of the chart.

▶ Compare Prisms and Pyramids

Use the prisms you see below to complete the exercises.

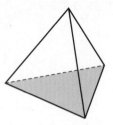

triangular pyramid

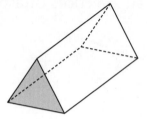

triangular prism

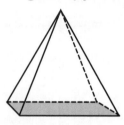

rectangular pyramid

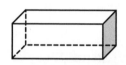

rectangular prism

20. How are pyramids and prisms named? Give an example
to support your answer.

_____

_____

_____

21. How are pyramids and prisms alike? Describe two ways.

_____

_____

_____

22. How are pyramids and prisms different? Describe two ways.

_____

_____

_____

Name _____ **Date** _____

Name the solid.

1.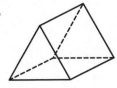

   _____

2.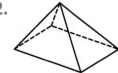

   _____

Find the number of faces, edges, and vertices in the solids above.

3. Exercise 1: _____ faces   _____ edges   _____ vertices

4. Exercise 2: _____ faces   _____ edges   _____ vertices

Find the surface area of the prism.

5. *Show your work.*

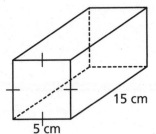

15 cm

5 cm

surface area = _____

6.

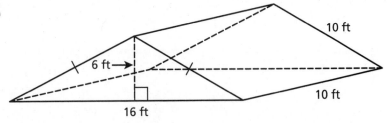

10 ft

6 ft→

16 ft

10 ft

surface area = _____

Name the solid that you can make from the net.

7.

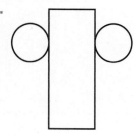

_____

8.

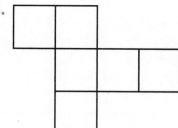

_____

9.

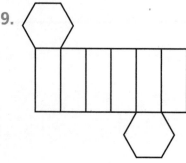

_____

10. **Extended Response** How are a cylinder and a triangular prism alike? How are they different? List two reasons for each.

_____

_____

_____

_____

_____

Name _____   Date _____

▶ Tenths and Hundredths

Pennies and dimes can help you understand tenths and hundredths. Discuss what you see.

100 pennies = 10 dimes = 1 dollar

100 pennies = 1 dollar   10 dimes = 1 dollar

1 penny is $\frac{1}{100}$ of a dollar   1 dime is $\frac{1}{10}$ of a dollar

1.   1 penny = $\frac{1}{100}$ = 0.01

$\frac{10}{100}$ 10 of 100 equal parts

$\frac{1}{10}$ 1 of 10 equal parts

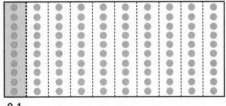

0.1
0.10

2.   1 dime = $\frac{1}{10}$ = 0.1

$\frac{10}{100} + \frac{10}{100} = \frac{20}{100}$

$\frac{1}{10} + \frac{1}{10} = \frac{2}{10}$

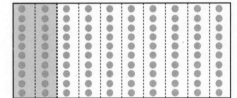

0.1 + 0.1 = 0.2
0.10 + 0.10 = 0.20

3. $\frac{10}{100} + \frac{10}{100} + \frac{5}{100} = \frac{25}{100}$

$\frac{1}{10} + \frac{1}{10} + \frac{5}{100} = \frac{25}{100}$

0.1 + 0.1 + 0.05 = 0.25
0.10 + 0.10 + 0.05 = 0.25

4. $\frac{25}{100} + \frac{25}{100} + \frac{25}{100} = \frac{75}{100}$

0.25 + 0.25 + 0.25 = 0.75

5. $\frac{1}{10} + \frac{1}{10} + \frac{1}{10} + \frac{1}{10} + \frac{1}{10} = \frac{5}{10} = \frac{1}{2}$

0.1 + 0.1 + 0.1 + 0.1 + 0.1 = 0.5
0.10 + 0.10 + 0.10 + 0.10 + 0.10 = 0.50

Name _____   **Date** _____

▶ Halves and Fourths

Equal shares of 1 whole can be written as a fraction or as a decimal. Each whole dollar below is equal to 100 pennies. Discuss the patterns you see.

6.

$\frac{1}{2}$ 1 of 2 equal parts

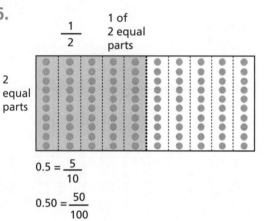

2 equal parts

$0.5 = \frac{5}{10}$

$0.50 = \frac{50}{100}$

7. $\frac{1}{2} + \frac{1}{2} = \frac{2}{2}$ 2 of 2 equal parts $= 1$ whole

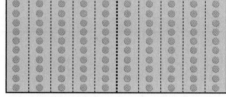

$0.5 + 0.5 = 1.00 = \frac{5}{10} + \frac{5}{10} = \frac{10}{10}$

$0.50 + 0.50 = 1.00 = \frac{50}{100} + \frac{50}{100} = \frac{100}{100}$

8.

$\frac{1}{4}$ 1 of 4 equal parts

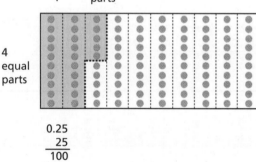

4 equal parts

0.25

$\frac{25}{100}$

9. $\frac{1}{4} + \frac{1}{4} = \frac{2}{4}$ 2 of 4 equal parts

$0.25 + 0.25 = 0.50$

$\frac{25}{100} + \frac{25}{100} = \frac{50}{100}$

10. $\frac{1}{4} + \frac{1}{4} + \frac{1}{4} = \frac{3}{4}$ 3 of 4 equal parts

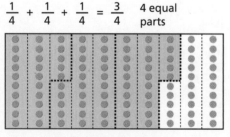

$0.25 + 0.25 + 0.25 = 0.75$

$\frac{25}{100} + \frac{25}{100} + \frac{25}{100} = \frac{75}{100}$

11. $\frac{1}{4} + \frac{1}{4} + \frac{1}{4} + \frac{1}{4} = \frac{4}{4}$ 4 of 4 equal parts $= 1$ whole

$0.25 + 0.25 + 0.25 + 0.25 = 1.00$

$\frac{25}{100} + \frac{25}{100} + \frac{25}{100} + \frac{25}{100} = \frac{100}{100}$

Vocabulary
mixed number

▶ Numbers Greater Than 1

Numbers greater than 1 can be written as fractions, decimals, or mixed numbers. A **mixed number** is a number that is represented by a whole number and a fraction.

Discuss the patterns you see in the equivalent fractions, decimals, and mixed numbers shown below.

12. $\frac{1}{4} + \frac{1}{4} + \frac{1}{4} + \frac{1}{4} + \frac{1}{4} = \frac{5}{4}$ 5 of 4 equal parts $= 1\frac{1}{4}$

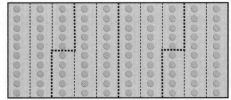 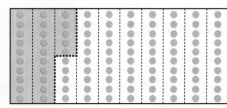

$\frac{4}{4} + \frac{1}{4}$

0.25 + 0.25 + 0.25 + 0.25 + 0.25 = 1.25

$\frac{25}{100} + \frac{25}{100} + \frac{25}{100} + \frac{25}{100} + \frac{25}{100} = \frac{125}{100} = 1\frac{25}{100}$

13. $\frac{1}{4} + \frac{1}{4} + \frac{1}{4} + \frac{1}{4} + \frac{1}{4} + \frac{1}{4} = \frac{6}{4}$ 6 of 4 equal parts $= 1\frac{2}{4}$

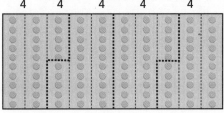 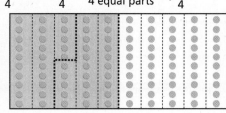

$\frac{4}{4} + \frac{2}{4}$

0.25 + 0.25 + 0.25 + 0.25 + 0.25 + 0.25 = 1.50

$\frac{25}{100} + \frac{25}{100} + \frac{25}{100} + \frac{25}{100} + \frac{25}{100} + \frac{25}{100} = \frac{150}{100} = \frac{100}{100} + \frac{50}{100} = 1 + \frac{50}{100} = 1\frac{50}{100}$

14. $\frac{1}{4} + \frac{1}{4} + \frac{1}{4} + \frac{1}{4} + \frac{1}{4} + \frac{1}{4} + \frac{1}{4} = \frac{7}{4}$ 7 of 4 equal parts $= 1\frac{3}{4}$

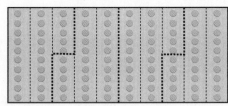 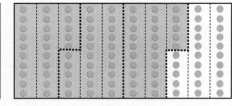

$\frac{4}{4} + \frac{3}{4}$

0.25 + 0.25 + 0.25 + 0.25 + 0.25 + 0.25 + 0.25 = 1.75

$\frac{25}{100} + \frac{25}{100} + \frac{25}{100} + \frac{25}{100} + \frac{25}{100} + \frac{25}{100} + \frac{25}{100} = \frac{175}{100} = \frac{100}{100} + \frac{75}{100} = 1 + \frac{75}{100} = 1\frac{75}{100}$

Class Activity

▶ Represent Equivalent Fractions and Decimals

Write a fraction and a decimal to represent the shaded part of each whole.

15.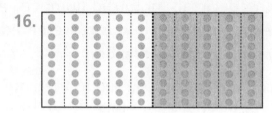

_____

16.

_____

Divide each whole and use shading to show the given fraction or decimal.

17. 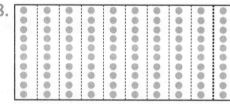   0.75

_____

18. 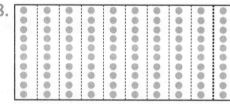 $\frac{9}{10}$

_____

Shade these grids to show that $\frac{3}{2} = 1\frac{1}{2}$.

19.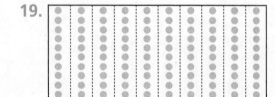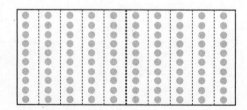

Relate Fractions and Decimals

Vocabulary

tenths
hundredths
decimal number

▶ Understand Tenths and Hundredths

Answer the questions about the bars and number lines below.

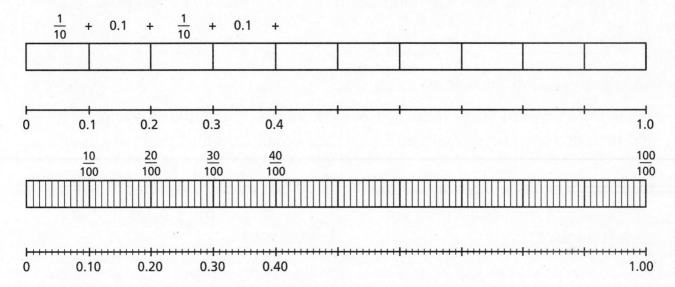

$\frac{1}{10}$ + 0.1 + $\frac{1}{10}$ + 0.1 +

0   0.1   0.2   0.3   0.4   1.0

$\frac{10}{100}$ $\frac{20}{100}$ $\frac{30}{100}$ $\frac{40}{100}$ $\frac{100}{100}$

0   0.10   0.20   0.30   0.40   1.00

1. The bars show **tenths** and **hundredths**. Finish labeling the bars and number lines using fractions and **decimal numbers**.

2. Use what you know about fractions and about money (a dime = one tenth of a dollar and a penny = one hundredth of a dollar) to explain why 3 tenths is the same as 30 hundredths.

_____

_____

_____

3. Tenths are larger than hundredths even though 10 is a smaller number than 100. Explain why this is true.

_____

_____

Class Activity

▶ Practice Writing Decimal Numbers

Write these numbers in decimal form.

4. 8 tenths _____   5. 6 hundredths _____   6. 35 hundredths _____

7. $\frac{92}{100}$ _____   8. $\frac{2}{10}$ _____   9. $\frac{9}{100}$ _____

Answer the questions below.

In the little town of Silver there are 100 people. Four are left-handed.

10. What decimal number shows the fraction of the people who are left-handed?

_____

11. What decimal number shows the fraction of the people who are right-handed?

_____

There are 10 children playing volleyball, and 6 of them are boys.

12. What decimal number shows the fraction of the players that are boys?

_____

13. What decimal number shows the fraction of the players that are girls?

_____

Complete the table.

	Name of Coin	Fraction of a Dollar	Decimal Part of a Dollar
14.	Penny	$\frac{}{100}$	
15.	Nickel	$\frac{}{100} =$	
16.	Dime	$\frac{}{100} =$	
17.	Quarter	$\frac{}{100} =$	

Name _____   Date _____

▶ **Decimal Secret Code Cards**

0.1	0.01
0.1	**0.01**
0.2	0.02
0.2	**0.02**
0.3	0.03
0.3	**0.03**
0.4	0.04
0.4	**0.04**
0.5	0.05
0.5	**0.05**
0.6	0.06
0.6	**0.06**
0.7	0.07
0.7	**0.07**
0.8	0.08
0.8	**0.08**
0.9	0.09
0.9	**0.09**

.00

.00

.00

.00

> <

Class Activity

Name _____ **Date** _____

▶ Decimal Secret Code Cards

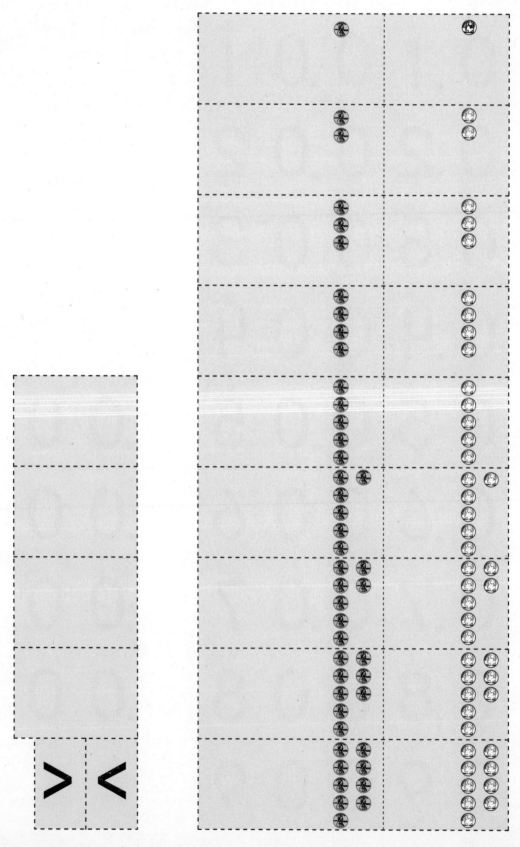

Decimal Secret Code Cards

Dear Family,

In this unit, your child will be introduced to decimal numbers. Students will explore decimal numbers by using bars divided into tenths and hundredths. They will relate decimals to fractions, which are also used to represent parts of a whole.

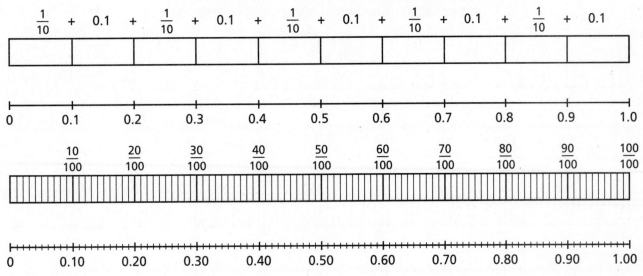

Students will also learn to combine whole numbers with decimals. They will work with numbers such as 1.72 and 12.9. They will round decimal numbers. For example, 0.87 rounded to the nearest tenth is 0.9. Students will also compare decimal numbers with other decimal numbers and with fractions. They will compare decimal numbers with fractions as well.

Students will apply their understanding of decimal concepts when they add or compare decimals.

Adding Decimals

3.9 + 2.21

$$\begin{array}{r} \overset{1}{3.9} \\ + 2.21 \\ \hline 6.11 \end{array}$$

Be sure to remind your child to line up the decimals.

Comparing Decimals

6.8 ◯ 3.42   6.80 ⟩ 3.42

Adding a zero makes the numbers easier to compare.

Please call if you have any questions or comments.

Thank you.

Sincerely,
Your child's teacher

Estimada familia:

En esta unidad su niño verá por primera vez los números decimales. Los estudiantes explorarán los números decimales usando barras divididas en décimas y centésimas. También relacionarán los decimales con las fracciones, ya que las fracciones también representan partes de un entero.

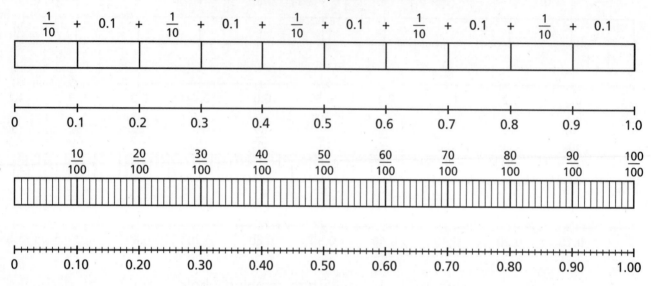

Los estudiantes también aprenderán a combinar números enteros con decimales. Trabajarán con números como 1.72 y 12.9, y redondearán números decimales. Por ejemplo, 0.87 redondeado a la décima más cercana es 0.9. Los estudiantes también compararán los números decimales con otros números decimales. Además, compararán números decimales con fracciones. Por ejemplo, 0.45 es un poco menos de la mitad y $\frac{7}{12}$ es un poco más de la mitad, por lo que $\frac{7}{12}$ es mayor que 0.45.

Los estudiantes aplicarán su comprensión de conceptos decimales al sumar o comparar decimales.

Sumar decimales

3.9 + 2.21

$$\begin{array}{r} \overset{1}{3.9} \\ + 2.21 \\ \hline 6.11 \end{array}$$

Asegúrese de recordar a su niño que debe alinear los decimales.

Comparar decimales

6.8 $\bigcirc$ 3.42

6.80 $(>)$ 3.42

Añadir un cero facilita la comparación de números.

Si tiene alguna duda o comentario, por favor comuníquese conmigo.

Gracias.

Atentamente,
El maestro de su niño

Explore Decimal Numbers

Name _____   **Date** _____

Class Activity

▶ Write Decimal Numbers

In the situations below, each person is traveling the same distance. Write a decimal number to represent the distance each person has traveled.

1. Aki has traveled 3 tenths of the distance, and Steven has traveled 5 tenths of the distance.

   Aki _____   Steven _____

2. Jose has traveled 25 hundredths of the distance, and Lakisha has traveled 18 hundredths of the distance.

   Jose _____   Lakisha _____

3. Yasir has traveled 7 tenths of the distance, and Danielle has traveled 59 hundredths of the distance.

   Yasir _____   Danielle _____

4. Lea has traveled 8 hundredths of the distance, and Kwang-Sun has traveled 6 tenths of the distance.

   Lea _____   Kwang-Sun _____

▶ Practice Comparing

Write <, >, or = to compare these numbers.

5. 0.4 ◯ 0.04   6. 0.30 ◯ 0.3   7. 0.7 ◯ 0.24   8. 0.1 ◯ 0.8

9. 0.61 ◯ 0.8   10. 0.54 ◯ 0.2   11. 0.11 ◯ 0.15   12. 0.02 ◯ 0.2

13. 0.5 ◯ 0.50   14. 0.77 ◯ 0.3   15. 0.06 ◯ 0.6   16. 0.9 ◯ 0.35

17. 0.4 ◯ 0.7   18. 0.1 ◯ 0.10   19. 0.5 ◯ 0.81   20. 0.41 ◯ 0.39

21. 0.9 ◯ 0.09   22. 0.48 ◯ 0.6   23. 0.53 ◯ 0.4   24. 0.70 ◯ 0.7

▶ Word Problems With Decimal Numbers

Solve.

The Cruz family is enjoying a 10-day vacation. So far, they have been vacationing for one week.

25. What decimal number represents the part of their vacation that is past? _____

26. What decimal number represents the part of their vacation that remains? _____

Jeremy spent 3 quarters and 1 nickel at the school bookstore.

27. What decimal part of a dollar did he spend?

_____

28. What decimal part of a dollar did he not spend?

_____

Dana is planning to run 1 tenth of a mile every day for 8 days.

29. What part of a mile will she have run at the end of the eighth day? _____

30. How many more days must she run to reach a mile?

_____

▶ Practice Writing Decimal Numbers

Write the word name of each number.

31. 0.1 _____   32. 0.73 _____

33. 0.09 _____   34. 0.5 _____

Write a decimal number for each word name.

35. fourteen hundredths   36. two tenths _____

_____

37. eight tenths _____   38. six hundredths _____

Compare Decimals to Hundredths

Class Activity

Name _____   Date _____

▶ Discuss Symmetry Around the Ones

◀───── ×10 ─────   **Place Value Chart** ───── ÷10 ─────▶

Hundreds	Tens	ONES	Tenths	Hundredths
100.	10.	1.	0.1	0.01
$\frac{100}{1}$	$\frac{10}{1}$	$\frac{1}{1}$	$\frac{1}{10}$	$\frac{1}{100}$
🏛️$100	🏛️$10	🏛️$1	🪙	🪙

1. Discuss symmetries and relationships you see in the place value chart.

2. Is it easier to see place value patterns in **a** or **b**? Discuss why.

   a. 500   50   5   .5   .05

   b. 500   50   5   0.5   0.05

Use your Decimal Secret Code Cards to make numbers on the frame.

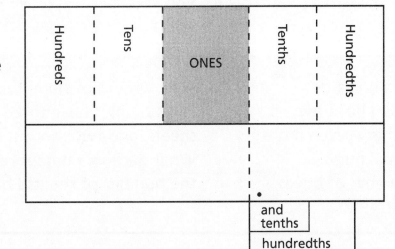

Class Activity

▶ Practice Hundreds to Hundredths

Write each mixed number as a decimal.

3. $3\frac{1}{10}$ _____

4. $5\frac{7}{100}$ _____

5. $2\frac{46}{100}$ _____

6. $28\frac{9}{10}$ _____

Write each decimal as a mixed number.

7. 12.8 _____

8. 3.05 _____

9. 4.85 _____

10. 49.7 _____

Write a decimal for each word name.

11. sixty-one hundredths

_____

12. six and fourteen hundredths

_____

13. seventy and eight tenths

_____

14. fifty-five and six hundredths

_____

Write <, >, or = to compare these numbers.

15. 27.5 ◯ 8.37   16. 6.04 ◯ 5.98   17. 7.36 ◯ 7.38   18. 36.9 ◯ 37.8

19. 0.5 ◯ 0.26   20. 0.09 ◯ 0.9   21. 0.8 ◯ 0.80   22. 0.42 ◯ 0.6

Solve.

23. A new box of trading cards contains 100 cards. I have two new boxes, and thirty-seven more cards. What decimal number represents the number of boxes I have?

_____

24. A new sheet of stamps contains 100 stamps. I have three new sheets, and two more stamps. What decimal number represents the number of sheets I have?

_____

Relate Whole Numbers and Decimals

Class Activity

Name

Date

► Secret Code Cards

100 1 0 0	10 1 0	1 1
200 2 0 0	20 2 0	2 2
300 3 0 0	30 3 0	3 3
400 4 0 0	40 4 0	4 4
500 5 0 0	50 5 0	5 5
600 6 0 0	60 6 0	6 6
700 7 0 0	70 7 0	7 7
800 8 0 0	80 8 0	8 8
900 9 0 0	90 9 0	9 9

▶ Secret Code Cards

| $1 | $10 | | $100 |
| $1 | $10 | | $100 |

(Decimal Secret Code Cards grid of $1, $10, and $100 denomination cards)

Class Activity

▶ Discuss Symmetry Around the Ones

	× 10		Place Value Chart		÷ 10	
Thousands	Hundreds	Tens	ONES	Tenths	Hundredths	Thousandths
1,000.	100.	10.	1.	0.1	0.01	0.001
$\frac{1,000}{1}$	$\frac{100}{1}$	$\frac{10}{1}$	$\frac{1}{1}$	$\frac{1}{10}$	$\frac{1}{100}$	$\frac{1}{1,000}$

25. Are the symmetries around the ones place also true for the thousands and thousandths places? Discuss why or why not.

Write the equivalent number of hundredths and thousandths.

26. 0.2 = _____ = _____

27. 0.8 = _____ = _____

28. 0.9 = _____ = _____

29. 0.6 = _____ = _____

Use your Decimal Secret Code Cards to make numbers on the

Place value	Thousands	Hundreds	Tens	ONES	Tenths	Hundredths	Thousandths
Make numbers							

Read numbers

| and tenths |
| hundredths |
| thousandths |

▶ Practice Thousands to Thousandths

Write each mixed number as a decimal.

30. $6\frac{3}{100}$ _____

31. $12\frac{705}{1,000}$ _____

32. $41\frac{4}{1,000}$ _____

33. $7\frac{9}{10}$ _____

Write each decimal as a mixed number.

34. 26.312 _____

35. 2.1 _____

36. 3.88 _____

37. 8.450 _____

Write a decimal for each word name.

38. five tenths

_____

39. nine and one thousandth

_____

40. ten and two hundredths

_____

41. six hundred eight thousandths

_____

Write <, >, or = to compare these numbers.

42. 23.1 ◯ 20.8

43. 0.105 ◯ 0.150

44. 4.55 ◯ 4.05

45. 0.1 ◯ 0.100

46. 3.1 ◯ 2.979

47. 1.40 ◯ 1.4

48. 0.108 ◯ 0.180

49. 7.300 ◯ 7.30

Solve.

50. A new container of hobby beads contains 1,000 beads. Sara has 1 new container, and 14 leftover beads. What decimal number represents the number of containers Sara has?

_____

51. A new container of hobby beads contains 1,000 beads. Wia has $2\frac{1}{2}$ new containers. Write three different decimal numbers to represent the number of containers Wia has.

_____

▶ Decimal Secret Code Cards

1,000 **1,0 0 0**	0.001 **0.0 0 1**
2,000 **2,0 0 0**	0.002 **0.0 0 2**
3,000 **3,0 0 0**	0.003 **0.0 0 3**
4,000 **4,0 0 0**	0.004 **0.0 0 4**
5,000 **5,0 0 0**	0.005 **0.0 0 5**
6,000 **6,0 0 0**	0.006 **0.0 0 6**
7,000 **7,0 0 0**	0.007 **0.0 0 7**
8,000 **8,0 0 0**	0.008 **0.0 0 8**
9,000 **9,0 0 0**	0.009 **0.0 0 9**

0 0 0

0.0 0 0

0.0 0 0

0.

Name _____ **Date** _____

► Decimal Secret Code Cards

▷ $1,000

▷▷ $1,000
$1,000

▷▷▷ $1,000
$1,000
$1,000

▷▷▷▷ $1,000
$1,000
$1,000
$1,000

▷▷▷▷▷ $1,000
$1,000
$1,000
$1,000
$1,000

▷▷▷▷▷▷ $1,000 $1,000
$1,000
$1,000
$1,000
$1,000

▷▷▷▷▷▷▷ $1,000 $1,000
$1,000 $1,000
$1,000
$1,000
$1,000

▷▷▷▷▷▷▷▷ $1,000 $1,000
$1,000 $1,000
$1,000 $1,000
$1,000
$1,000

▷▷▷▷▷▷▷▷▷ $1,000 $1,000
$1,000 $1,000
$1,000 $1,000
$1,000 $1,000
$1,000

Decimal Secret Code Cards

Name _____ **Date** _____

▶ Zeros in Greater Decimal Numbers

Use the tables to answer problems 1–4.

1. What happens if we insert a zero to the right of a whole number?

   _____

2. What happens if we insert a zero to the right of a decimal number?

   _____

Insert Zeros to the Right

Whole Numbers			Decimal Numbers		
3	30	300	0.3	0.30	0.300
52	520	5200	0.52	0.520	0.5200
67	670	6700	6.7	6.70	6.700

3. What happens if we insert a zero to the left of a whole number?

   _____

4. What happens if we insert a zero to the left of a decimal number just after the decimal point?

   _____

Insert Zeros to the Left

Whole Numbers			Decimal Numbers		
3	03	003	0.3	0.03	0.003
52	052	0052	0.52	0.052	0.0052
67	067	0067	6.7	6.07	6.007

5. Are whole numbers and decimal numbers alike or different when it comes to putting in extra zeros? Explain your answer.

   _____

   _____

   _____

   _____

6. Do the pairs of numbers below have the same value? Why or why not?

   0.6 and .6 _____   .25 and 0.25 _____   0.178 and .178 _____

   _____

▶ Adding Decimal Zeros

Cathy had to compare some decimal numbers. She used what she knew about adding zeros to decimal fractions without changing their value. Discuss why her solution is correct.

Problem:	**Solution:**
Which of these numbers is the greatest: 0.35, 0.318, or 0.4?	0.350 With the places aligned and 0.318 the extra zeros added, we 0.400 can see which is greatest.

Insert < or > to make a true statement.

7. 0.36 ◯ 0.82   8. 0.405 ◯ 0.62   9. 0.98 ◯ 0.7   10. 2.3 ◯ 0.95

11. 0.626 ◯ 0.65   12. 1.2 ◯ 0.85   13. 0.7 ◯ 0.07   14. 0.54 ◯ 0.504

15. The table shows the lengths of some common insects in inches. List the insects in order from largest to smallest.

Largest   _____

        _____

        _____

        _____

Smallest   _____

Size of Common Insects

Name	Length
Ladybug	0.25 in.
Aphid	0.062 in.
Mosquito	0.125 in.
Cricket	0.725 in.
Bumblebee	0.8 in.

Circle the number in each group that does *not* have the same value as the others.

16. .29   .290   .209   0.29   17. 0.7   .70 $\frac{7}{10}$ .07

18. .610   .601   0.61   .61   19. 4.8   4.80   4.08   4.800

Class Activity

Name _____ **Date** _____

▶ Round With Decimal Tenths and Hundredths

Vocabulary

tenths
hundredths
round

The number line below shows one whole divided into **tenths**.

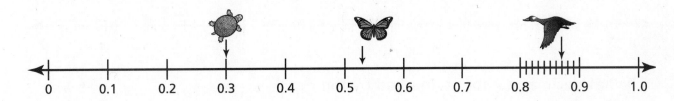

1. What decimal tenth is marked by the turtle? _____

Rounding Frames

2. The butterfly is between two decimal tenths. To which tenth is it nearer? _____

0.6

0.5

3. The bird is also between two decimal tenths. The space between these tenths has been divided into hundredths. What decimal **hundredths** are between 0.8 and 0.9?

_____

0.9
0.87
0.8

4. What decimal hundredth is marked by the bird? _____

5. To which tenth is this hundredth nearer? (This is the way you **round** a hundredth to the nearest tenth.) _____

The number line below shows one whole divided into hundredths.

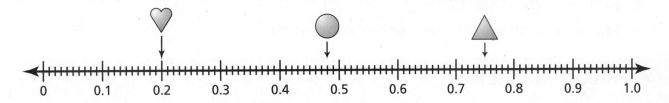

6. What hundredth is marked by the circle? _____

   Round this hundredth to the nearest tenth. _____

0.5
0.48
0.4

7. When you want to round a number that is exactly halfway between two rounding units, round up to the next greater number. What number is marked by the triangle? _____

   Round this number to the nearest tenth. _____

0.8
0.75
0.7

Class Activity

Name _____ **Date** _____

▶ Round Numbers Greater Than One

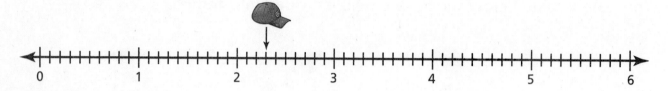

8. What decimal number is marked by the hat? _____

    Round this number to the nearest whole number. _____

9. Find 4.5 on the number line. Put an arrow there.

    What is 4.5 rounded to the nearest whole number? _____

    What is 4.5 expressed as decimal hundredths? _____

The ruler below shows centimeters and tenths of a centimeter.

10. How long is the string above the ruler? _____

11. How long is the string below the ruler to the nearest
    tenth of a centimeter? _____
    Round your answer to the nearest centimeter. _____

▶ Practice Rounding

Round to the nearest tenth.

12. 0.72 _____   13. 0.35 _____

14. 0.91 _____   15. 2.09 _____

16. What is $0.56 rounded to the
    nearest tenth of a dollar (dime)?

    _____

Round to the nearest whole number.

17. 3.8 _____   18. 32.7 _____

19. 12.5 _____   20. 8.24 _____

21. What is $7.28 rounded to the
    nearest dollar? _____

Class Activity

Name

Date

▶ Number Lines and Whole Numbers

Each point on a number line represents a number. Estimate the position of each whole number on the number line below. Plot and label a point for each number.

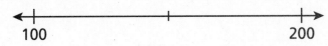

100   200

1. 160   2. 119   3. 176   4. 135   5. 191

▶ Number Lines and Fractions

Estimate the position of each fraction on the number line below. Plot and label a point for each fraction.

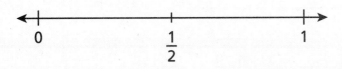

0 $\frac{1}{2}$ 1

6. $\frac{4}{8}$ 7. $\frac{1}{4}$ 8. $\frac{3}{4}$ 9. $\frac{7}{8}$ 10. $\frac{7}{16}$

▶ Number Lines and Mixed Numbers

Estimate the position of each mixed number on the number line below. Plot and label a point for each mixed number.

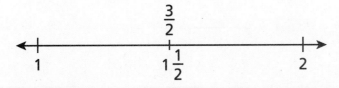

1 $\frac{3}{2}$ 2
        $1\frac{1}{2}$

11. $1\frac{1}{4}$ 12. $1\frac{3}{4}$ 13. $1\frac{7}{8}$ 14. $1\frac{1}{8}$ 15. $1\frac{13}{16}$

Class Activity

▶ Number Lines and Decimals

Estimate the position of each decimal number on the number line below. Plot and label a point for each number.

```
 ←———┼——————————————————————┼———→
     1                      2
```

16. 1.5   **17.** 1.1   **18.** 1.96   **19.** 1.65   **20.** 1.37

▶ Represent Numbers on a Number Line

Estimate the position of each number on the number line below. Plot and label a point for each number.

```
 ←———┼——————————————————————┼———→
     0                      2
```

21. $1\frac{3}{8}$ **22.** 1.24   **23.** $\frac{2}{3}$ **24.** 0.73   **25.** $1\frac{4}{5}$

26. In the space below, use a ruler and draw a number line. Place at least two tick marks with labels on the number line. Write three numbers that can be placed on the number line. Then challenge a classmate to plot the numbers.

▶ Real-World Applications

Solve.

1. Samantha has a quarter, a dime, and 2 pennies in her pocket. What decimal part of a dollar does she have?

_____

2. Today the Grade 4 runners ran 0.71 kilometers. The Grade 6 runners ran 0.675 kilometers. Which team ran farther?

_____

3. Oliver is building a patio with flat stones. He has decided to use only stones that are between 0.75 and 0.9 meters across. Below is a list of the measurements of the stones he has gathered so far. Check the ones he can use.

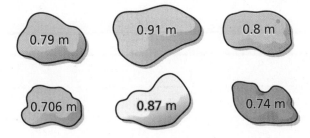

0.79 m   0.91 m   0.8 m

0.706 m   0.87 m   0.74 m

4. Chad is 1.78 meters tall. His friend Rob is 1.8 meters tall, and his friend Brent is 1.735 meters tall. Make a chart showing their heights rounded to the nearest hundredth. List the rounded heights in order from tallest to shortest.

_____

_____

_____

5. **On the Back** Answer the Puzzled Penguin's letter.

Dear Math Students:

I have some squash seeds and tomato seeds to plant, but I don't know which is which. My garden book says that squash seeds are about 0.7 of a centimeter long, and tomato seeds are about 0.25 of a centimeter long. Since 25 is bigger than 7, I would say that the tomato seed is the bigger seed. My friend says that's wrong.

Who is right? Can you explain why?

Thank you.

Puzzled Penguin

Practice With Decimal Numbers

Class Activity

Name _____ Date _____

▶ Add Unlike Units

What's Wrong? The solutions below are not correct.
Explain why and correct each answer.

1. $23 + 10¢ = $33

_____

_____

2. 5 feet + 12 inches = 17 feet

_____

_____

3. 4 hours + 3 minutes = 7 hours

_____

_____

4. $\frac{2}{3} + \frac{3}{4} = \frac{5}{7}$

_____

_____

5. 0.6 + 0.05 = 0.11

_____

_____

6. 14 + 0.3 = 17

_____

_____

▶ Unlike Units on the Number Line

Use the number line to add the numbers.

7. 4 + 0.8 = _____   8. 2 + 0.3 = _____   9. 3 + 1.9 = _____

Circle the correctly aligned problem in each pair and solve it.

10. A. 1 2.5
        + 0.3

    B.   12.5
        + 0.3

11. A.   0.9
        + 0.56

    B.   0.9
        + 0.56

12. A.   2.15
        + 1.3

    B.   2.15
        + 1.3

13. A.   0.734
        + 0.68

    B.   0.734
        + 0.68

▶ Align Decimal Numbers to Add

Add.

14. $48 + 12¢ =

15. 0.3 + 0.03 =

16. 23 + 0.36 =

17. $32.05 + 63¢ =

18. 0.25 + 0.18 =

19. 87.3 + 0.49 =

20. 16¢ + $5.27 =

21. 0.006 + 0.07 =

22. 72.17 + 1.5 =

▶ Solve Problems Involving Adding Decimal Numbers

Solve.

23. Roberto grew 0.96 centimeters last year and 0.8 centimeters the year before. How many centimeters did Roberto grow in two years?

24. Colleen and Jack both delivered newspapers this summer. Colleen earned $103.26 and Jack earned $92.12. How much did they earn together?

25. Hannah has 6.721 liters of lemonade. She will mix it with 3.44 liters of raspberry juice to make raspberry lemonade. How many liters of raspberry lemonade will Hannah have?

26. Last year Maria's oak tree was 4.5 meters tall. This year it grew 0.41 meters. How tall is the oak tree now?

Add Decimal Numbers

► Order Decimal Numbers to Subtract

Find the difference between each pair of numbers.

1. 0.89 and 0.7

2. 0.09 and 0.23

3. 0.837 and 0.2

4. 0.006 and 0.35

5. 1.04 and 0.7

6. 3.56 and 0.008

► Solve Problems Involving Decimal Number Subtraction

Solve.

7. Rosa had a rope 6.5 meters long. She cut off a piece 1.45 meters long to make a jump rope. How much rope does Rosa have left?

8. A robin's egg is about 1.35 centimeters long. A hummingbird's egg is about 0.6 centimeters long. How much longer is a robin's egg?

9. A turtle can travel 0.17 miles per hour. A snail can travel 0.032 miles per hour. Which animal can move faster? _____ How much faster? _____

10. Ramona had $26. She spent 35 cents to buy a pencil. How much money does Ramona have now?

► Decimals on the Map

Use the map to answer the questions 11–13.

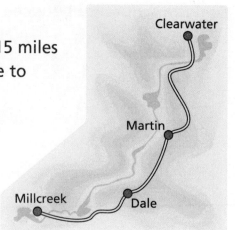

11. If it is 17.5 miles from Millcreek to Dale and 33.15 miles from Millcreek to Martin, how far is it from Dale to Martin? _____

12. If it is 49 miles from Dale to Clearwater, how far is it from Martin to Clearwater?

    _____

13. How far is the entire distance from Millcreek to Clearwater? _____

► Decimal Word Problems

Solve.

Show your work.

14. Mr. Kelly raises honeybees for a living. Today he collected 0.28 ounces of dark honey and 0.9 ounces of light honey. How many ounces of honey did Mr. Kelly collect today? _____

15. Mr. Kelly sells honey in two sizes. There is a 9.5-ounce jar and a 4.75-ounce jar. What is the difference in weight between the two jars?

    _____

16. Mr. Kelly has collected 0.85 ounces of honey today. How much more will he need to collect to fill a 4.75-ounce jar? _____

17. Last week Mr. Kelly sold a total of 41.75 ounces of light honey and 18.5 ounces of dark honey. How much honey did he sell last week?

    _____

Subtract Decimal Numbers

Name _____ **Date** _____

▶ Find Money Amounts

Cory earned the amount of money
shown on the right. How much money
did Cory earn? _____

Write each amount.

1.

_____

2.

_____

3.

_____

4.

_____

5. 4 quarters, 5 nickels _____

6. 4 nickels, 7 dimes, 8 quarters _____

7. 8 dimes, 3 pennies _____

8. 3 quarters, 1 half-dollar, 2 dimes _____

Solve.

9. How can you make $112
using the least number of bills?

_____

_____

10. How can you make forty-
nine cents using nine coins?

_____

_____

Making Change **449**

▶ Compare and Order Money Amounts

Circle the greater amount—A or B.

11. A.    B.

12. A.   B.

13. A. 6 dimes 3 quarters 5 nickels   B. 7 nickels 2 half-dollars

14. A. 2 hundred-dollar bills, 4 ten-dollar bills   B. 5 fifty-dollar bills

15. Write the amounts in order from greatest to least.

    $3.19 $2.44 $2.71 $3.11 _____

16. Write the amounts below in order from least to greatest.

    $62.50 $62.52 $60.99 $61.11 _____

Solve.

17. The students at Valley Middle School participated in a school fundraiser. The amount of money each class earned is shown in the table at the right.

    The goal of the students was to earn $500. Did the students reach their goal? Explain how you can use an estimate to help decide.

Valley School Fundraiser	
Grade 4	$160.50
Grade 5	$138.00
Grade 6	$171.25

_____

_____

Name _____   **Date** _____

▶ Make Change

A $5 bill was used to buy each item below. List the coins and bills you would use to make change.

18. $3.75

_____

_____

19.  $0.59

_____

_____

A $20 bill was used to buy each item below. List the coins and bills you would use to make change.

20.  $12.65

_____

_____

21.  $16.79

_____

_____

Write the names and numbers of coins and bills you would use to make change for each of the following.

22. The cost of an item is $3.59. You give the clerk 4 one-dollar bills.

_____

_____

23. The cost of an item is $1.09. You give the clerk 5 quarters.

_____

_____

24. The cost of an item is 27¢. You give the clerk a half-dollar.

_____

_____

25. The cost of an item is $4.15. You give the clerk five dollars.

_____

_____

Vocabulary

tenths
hundredths

▶ Patterns in Tenths and Hundredths

A decimal number in **tenths** has one digit to the right of the decimal point. A decimal number in **hundredths** has two digits to the right of the decimal point.

Place Value Chart			
ones	•	tenths	hundredths

Using words, describe each pattern of decimal numbers. Then write the next term in the sequence.

1. $0.55 $0.54 $0.53 $0.52 $0.51 _____

_____

_____

2. 1.5   1.6   1.7   1.8   1.9 _____

_____

_____

Write the next term in each sequence.

3. $12.18, $12.19, $12.20, $12.21, $12.22 _____

4. $4.59, $4.57, $4.55, $4.53, $4.51 _____

5. 3.9, 3.8, 3.7, 3.6, 3.5 _____

6. 8.5, 8.6, 8.7, 8.8, 8.9 _____

7. 79.1, 79.3, 79.5, 79.7, 79.9 _____

8. 32.5, 32, 31.5, 31, 30.5 _____

9. 6.35, 6.5, 6.65, 6.8, 6.95 _____

Making Change

Class Activity

Name _____   Date _____

Vocabulary

estimate

▶ Estimate With Decimal Numbers

Estimate the answers by rounding each number to the nearest tenth.

1. 0.83 + 0.121 _____

2. 0.64 − 0.07 _____

3. 0.09 + 0.8 _____

4. 0.75 − 0.18 _____

5. 3.41 + 1.29 _____

6. 1.50 − 0.79 _____

▶ The Puzzled Penguin

Dear Math Students:

I had $0.95 to spend at the store today. I wanted to buy a pen for $0.53 and some stickers for $0.44.

I rounded the price of the pen down to $0.50 and the price of the stickers down to $0.40. I thought I had enough because $0.50 + $0.40 is less than $0.95. But the cashier told me I didn't have enough. What did I do wrong?

Thank you.

Puzzled Penguin

_____

_____

_____

_____

Make a safe estimate to solve the problems.

7. Jenna wants to buy apple juice for $0.64 and a muffin for $0.98. She has $1.75. Does she have enough money?

_____

8. Pedro has 5 quarters. He wants to buy a pencil for $0.34 and a notebook for $0.93. Does he have enough money?

_____

▶ Round Different Ways in Different Contexts

The table shows how much money Jahmal earned this month selling newspapers. Use the table to answer the questions below.

Week 1	$19.68
Week 2	$ 8.92
Week 3	$28.95
Week 4	$10.16

9. Estimate Jahmal's total earnings by rounding to the nearest ten dollars.

_____

10. About how much more did Jahmal make in Week 1 than in Week 2? Estimate by rounding to the nearest dollar.

_____

11. About how much more did Jahmal make in Week 3 than in Week 4? Estimate by rounding to the nearest dollar.

_____

▶ Discuss Selecting a Rounding Unit

Select a rounding unit that allows you to estimate the answer mentally. Write your rounded problem and your estimated answer.

12. 0.429 + 0.502 _____

13. 1.85 − 0.9 _____

14. 0.88 − 0.283 _____

15. 0.59 − 0.19 _____

16. 3.678 + 4.123 _____

17. 2.69 + 0.3 _____

▶ Math Connection: Estimate With Metric Units

Solve the problems.

1. The length of each side of a square fence is
   8.6 meters. Estimate the total length of the fence.

   Show your work.

   _____

2. A quarter has a mass of 5.67 grams. A dime has a
   mass of 2.268 grams. Estimate their total mass.

   _____

3. Kimo bought two jars of juice. One jar had
   0.52 liters of juice. The other jar had 1 liter of juice.
   Estimate the difference in liters between the jars.

   _____

4. Shawn is painting a fence. He has 5 cans of paint.
   Each can has 3.784 liters of paint. Estimate how many
   liters of paint Shawn has in all.

   _____

5. Nina measured the mass of some apples at 1.34
   kilograms. She measured some pears at 1.09 kilograms.
   Estimate the total mass of the apples and pears.

   _____

6. The driving distance from Ida's home to Flo's home is
   184.19 kilometers. Ida divides the trip into 2 equal
   parts. Estimate how many kilometers Ida will travel
   for each part of the trip.

   _____

7. **On the Back** Arnette put ribbon around a picture frame.
   The length of the frame is 10.16 centimeters. The width
   of the frame is 15.24 centimeters. Estimate the total
   length of ribbon that is needed. Explain how you estimated.

Name Date

▶ Find the Difference

Find the difference between the numbers. Use mental math.

1. 0.99 and 0.11 _____   2. 0.006 and 0.356 _____   3. 0.07 and 0.27 _____

4. 1.59 and 0.5 _____   5. 0.835 and 0.1 _____   6. 1.00 and 4.68 _____

▶ Word Problems With Mixed Operations

Solve.

7. David's kite had a tail 1.5 meters long. David made it 0.75 meters longer. How long is the tail now?

_____

8. Magda had $35. She spent 73¢ to buy a bag of peanuts. How much money does Magda have now?

_____

9. Carlos feeds his hamsters 0.09 pounds of seeds mixed with 0.15 pounds of oatmeal every day. How many pounds of food do the hamsters get?

_____

10. The Crazy Curl roller coaster travels at 82.03 miles per hour (mph). The Big Drop travels at 82.015 mph. Which roller coaster is faster? How much faster?

_____

▶ Neighborhood Map Problems

Refer to the drawing. Estimate each answer by rounding the numbers to the nearest tenth.

11. How far is it from Justin's house to Dana's house? _____

12. How far does Ana have to walk to school?

_____

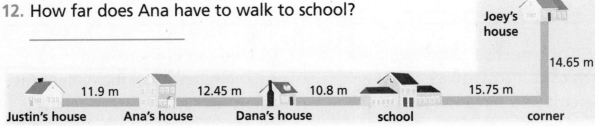

▶ Multiply Decimal Numbers

Solve

1. Ernesto is making a bookcase using wood. He cut a
   piece of wood into 4 equal pieces. Each cut piece was
   2.13 meters long. How long was the whole piece of
   wood he started with?

   _____

Multiply

2.	$0.74	3.	19.7	4.	0.37
	× 8		× 4		× 8

5.	$5.08	6.	0.982	7.	$6.17
	× 9		× 6		× 7

▶ Solve Problems by Multiplying Decimal Numbers

Solve.

8. Ms. Lindy bought 3 rolls of ribbon
   for wrapping gifts. The price of
   each roll was $2.16. What was the
   total cost of the 3 rolls?

   _____

9. Julie runs 1.35 miles each day.
   How many miles in all would she
   run if she ran for 5 days?

   _____

10. Mr. Cobb needs 6 cartons of juice.
    Each carton costs $0.89. What is
    the cost of 6 cartons?

    _____

11. Donnie can run $\frac{1}{2}$ mile in
    4.67 minutes. How many minutes
    will it take him to run 1 mile?

    _____

Mixed Practice With Decimals

► Fractions and Benchmarks

A number line can be used to estimate the sum of two or more fractions.

Decide if each fraction is closer to 0 or closer to 1. Write *closer to 0* or *closer to 1*.

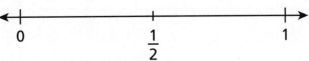

0          $\frac{1}{2}$ 1

1. $\frac{1}{4}$ _____

2. $\frac{3}{4}$ _____

3. $\frac{7}{8}$ _____

Decide if each addend is closer to 0 or closer to 1. Then estimate the sum.

4. $\frac{1}{8} + \frac{3}{4}$

Estimate: _____

5. $\frac{3}{4} + \frac{7}{8}$

Estimate: _____

6. $\frac{3}{10} + \frac{4}{5}$

Estimate: _____

► Decimals and Benchmarks

A number line can be used to estimate the sum of two or more decimals.

Decide if each decimal is closer to 0 or closer to 1. Write *closer to 0* or write *closer to 1*.

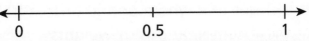

0   0.5   1

7. 0.4 _____

8. 0.9 _____

9. 0.6 _____

Decide if each addend is closer to 0.5, to 1, or to 1.5. Then estimate the sum.

10. 0.5 + 0.9

Estimate: _____

11. 0.8 + 0.11

Estimate: _____

12. 0.6 + 0.6

Estimate: _____

11–14

Class Activity

Name _____   **Date** _____

▶ Estimate With Fractions and Decimals

The list below shows a variety of cooking ingredients and amounts.

Ingredients and Amounts (c = cup)	
wheat flour $1\frac{5}{8}$ c	white flour $\frac{3}{4}$ c
sugar $1\frac{1}{4}$ c	cornstarch $\frac{3}{8}$ c

Decide if each amount is closer to $\frac{1}{2}$ cup, $1\frac{1}{2}$ cups or 2 cups. Then *estimate* the total of these amounts.

13. white flour + sugar _____

14. sugar + wheat flour _____

15. sugar + cornstarch _____

16. cornstarch + white flour _____

The list below shows a variety of packages and weights.

Packages To Be Shipped (lb = pounds)	
Package A 4.3 lb	Package B 5.6 lb
Package C 5.2 lb	Package D 4.8 lb

Decide if each weight is closer to a whole pound or to a half pound. Then *estimate* these combinations of weights.

17. A + B _____

18. C + B _____

19. B + D _____

20. D + A _____

21. What is a reasonable estimate of the total weight of all four packages? Explain your answer.

_____

_____

_____

Estimate Using Benchmarks

▶ Math and Art

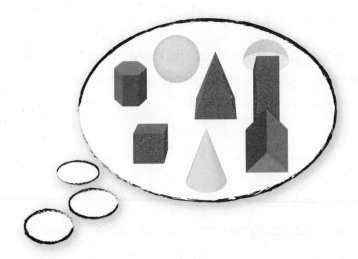

Imagine that you are asked to design a building that will be built 100 years from now. The only requirement is that the building be composed of at least three different geometric solids.

1. Before you start, think about the building. What will it be used for? Where will it be located?

   _____

   _____

2. On a separate piece of paper, draw a sketch of your building. You may want to use grid paper. Use your sketch to what your building will look like.

3. Once you have a final design, draw an illustration of your building on plain paper. Add color to it if you would like.

4. Write a description of your building. In the description, include the names of the geometric solids you used.

   _____

   _____

   _____

Name _____ **Date** _____

Class Activity

▶ Color a Map

Use the map of South America below or a copy of it.

1. Color each country on the map so that countries that are next to each other are not the same color. Use as *few* colors as possible.

2. How many colors did you use? What helped you decide?

_____

_____

Use Mathematical Processes

Name _____   **Date** _____

Write the number in decimal form.

1. sixty-four hundredths   **2.** $7\frac{3}{10}$ **3.** $12\frac{4}{100}$

_____   _____   _____

4. Write the decimal number in words.

   a. 23.01 _____

   b. 2.78 _____

Write >, <, or = to make a true statement.

5. 0.7 ◯ 0.75   **6.** 0.4 ◯ 0.25   **7.** 0.81 ◯ 0.89

8. Arrange these numbers in order from least to greatest.

   0.7   0.64   0.09   _____   _____   _____

Round to the nearest tenth and to the nearest whole number.

9. 0.87   nearest tenth: _____   nearest whole number: _____

10. 1.43   nearest tenth: _____   nearest whole number: _____

11. 2.67   nearest tenth: _____   nearest whole number: _____

Add or subtract.

12. 7.13 + 2.5   **13.** 8.36 − 4.78   **14.** 1.03 + 0.4   **15.** $26 − 15¢

16. Write the letter of the point that corresponds to each number.

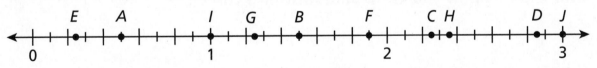

a. $1\frac{1}{4}$ _____   **b.** 0.5 _____   **c.** 2.35 _____   **d.** $1\frac{1}{2}$ _____   **e.** $1\frac{9}{10}$ _____

Solve.

Show your work.

17. On Monday, the average temperature was 29.7°F. On Tuesday, the average temperature was 37.64°F. How much warmer was it on Tuesday than on Monday?

_____

18. Jared's family drove 98.12 km to visit some cousins. Then they drove 85.3 km to visit some friends. How far did they travel altogether?

_____

19. Miguel spent $5.63 at the market. He gave the clerk $10.00.
   a. How much change will he receive?

_____

   b. List the least number of bills and coins Miguel will receive as change.

_____

20. **Extended Response** Tickets to an amusement park cost $27.99 for adults and $18.49 for children. Mrs. Ramirez has $47.00. Does she have enough money to buy tickets for herself and her 10-year-old son? Use a "safe estimate" to answer this question. Explain how you made your estimate and how you know your answer is correct.

_____

_____

_____

_____

_____

Class Activity

Name _____ **Date** _____

Vocabulary

| inch | yard |
| foot | mile |

▶ Units of Length

The inchworm gets its name because its method of crawling helps it move about an inch at a time.

1. This line segment is 1 **inch** long.
Hold up two fingers 1 inch apart.
Name an object that is about 1 inch long.

_____

2. One **foot** is equal to 12 inches. The line segment below is 1 foot long, but it has been folded into two 6-inch lengths.

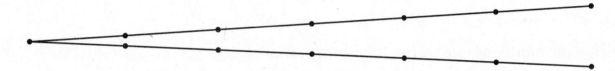

Spread your hands apart to show 1 foot. Name an object that is about 1 foot long. _____

3. Many years ago, people considered a distance of 1 foot to be the length of a person's foot. Measure the longest dimension of your classroom using your feet, and compare your results with those of your classmates. Why is using your feet not a good way to measure distance?

_____

_____

4. One **yard** is equal to 3 feet, or 36 inches. How many 6-inch lengths are equal to 1 yard?

_____

5. Longer distances are measured in miles. One **mile** is equal to 5,280 feet, or 1,760 yards. Why are feet and yards not used as often as miles when describing long distances?

_____

▶ Fractions of Length Units

Since 1 foot = 12 inches, this 6-inch ruler shows $\frac{1}{2}$ foot.

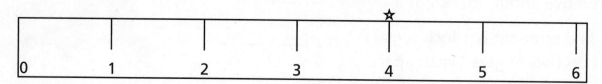

6. How many inches are between 0 and the star? _____

Use fractions in simplest form to complete the equations.

7. 1 in. = _____ ft   **8.** 3 in. = _____ ft   **9.** 4 in. = _____ ft

10. 1 ft = _____ yd   **11.** 2 ft = _____ yd

The shorter marks between the whole-inch marks represent the fractional parts. For each ruler below, what fraction of an inch is marked between the whole numbers? What measurement does the star show?

12.

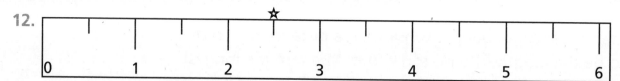

_____

13.

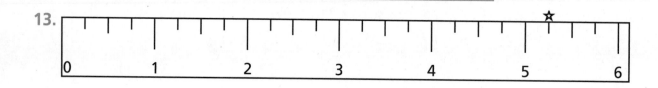

_____

14.

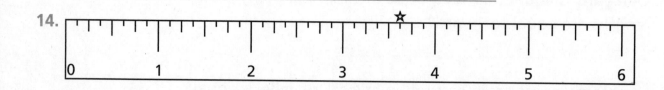

_____

15. Some rulers have shorter marks halfway between each $\frac{1}{8}$ mark. What fraction of an inch would these marks represent?

_____

Length

▶ Estimate and Measure Length

Estimate the length of each line segment. Then measure it to the nearest $\frac{1}{8}$ inch.

16. •————————————————•

_____

17. •——————————————————————•

_____

18. •————————————•

_____

19. •———————————•

_____

20. •——————————————————•

_____

Draw a line segment that has the given length.

21. $3\frac{3}{8}$ in.

22. $1\frac{3}{4}$ in.

23. $5\frac{1}{2}$ in.

24. $2\frac{1}{4}$ in.

25. $7\frac{6}{8}$ in.

Going Further

▶ Work Backward

Solve.

1. All of the students in a school are recording how far they ride their bicycles during the summer. They want to discover whether they ride enough miles altogether to equal the distance around the Earth. One day, Lola rode twice as far as Max and Max rode 5 more miles than Julia. If Julia rode 2 miles, how many miles altogether did the three riders contribute to the school's total on that day?

_____

2. Chandra spent half of her allowance for a theater ticket and $2.25 for popcorn. After the movie, she arrived home with $2.75. What was Chandra's allowance?

_____

3. Shelby's age is one-fourth Allison's age. Mito is 13 years old and 1 year older than Allison. How old is Shelby?

_____

4. Patrick gave one-third of a length of ribbon to Karin, and then divided the remaining ribbon equally with Jon. If Jon received 12 inches of ribbon, how many yards long was the ribbon Patrick began with?

_____

Dear Family,

In our math class, we are exploring different ways we measure things using our customary system of measurement.

Some of the units of measurement we will be working with include:

Length and Distance	Capacity
1 foot = 12 inches 1 yard = 3 feet 1 mile = 5,280 feet	1 cup = 8 fluid ounces 1 pint = 2 cups 1 quart = 2 pints 1 gallon = 4 quarts
Weight	Time
1 pound = 16 ounces 1 ton = 2,000 pounds	1 minute = 60 seconds 1 hour = 60 minutes 1 day = 24 hours 1 month = 28, 29, 30, or 31 days 1 year = 365 days leap year = 366 days

You can help your child become familiar with these units by finding examples together in your home and work. You might use a calendar to note that the number of days in each month is not always the same. You might use a measuring cup and explore how the cup can be used to make pints, quarts, or gallons of liquid. Or you might use a clock face to find "quarter to," "quarter after," and "half past" various hours. These activities and others will help your child better understand measurement.

If you have any questions, please call or write to me.

Sincerely,
Your child's teacher

Estimada familia:

En nuestra clase de matemáticas estamos explorando diferentes maneras de medir las cosas usando el sistema usual de medida.

Algunas de las unidades de medida con las que trabajaremos incluyen:

Longitud y distancia	Capacidad
1 pie = 12 pulgadas 1 yarda = 3 pies 1 milla = 5,280 pies	1 taza = 8 onzas líquidas 1 pinta = 2 tazas 1 cuarto = 2 pintas 1 galón = 4 cuartos
Peso	Tiempo
1 libra = 16 onzas 1 tonelada = 2,000 libras	1 minuto = 60 segundos 1 hora = 60 minutos 1 día = 24 horas 1 mes = 28, 29, 30 ó 31 días 1 año = 365 días 1 año bisiesto = 366 días

Será de gran ayuda si usted puede encontrar ejemplos de estas unidades en su casa y puede trabajar con su niño para que se familiarice con ellas. Por ejemplo, puede usar un calendario para hacerle notar que el número de días de cada mes no siempre es el mismo. Puede usar una taza de medir para explorar cómo la taza puede servir para hacer pintas, cuartos o galones. O puede usar la cara del reloj para hallar el "cuarto para" la hora, la hora "y cuarto" y la hora "y media" con diferentes horas. Estas y otras actividades van a ayudar a su niño a comprender las medidas.

Si tiene alguna pregunta, por favor comuníquese conmigo.

Atentamente,
El maestro de su niño

Length

Vocabulary

square inch
square foot
square yard

▶ Estimate Area

A square that measures 1 inch on each side is a **square inch**.
A square inch is used to measure area. Other units that are
used to measure area include a **square foot** and a
square yard.

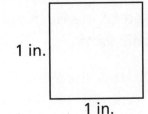

1 in.

1 in.

1. How many inches on each side does a square foot
   measure? How many square inches are equal to
   1 square foot?

   _____

2. How many feet on each side does a square yard measure?
   How many square feet are equal to 1 square yard?

   _____

3. Name something that might be measured in square inches.
   Name something that might be measured in square feet.
   Name something that might be measured in square yards.

   _____

   _____

Estimate area, and show your work.

4. Find the area in square inches of a rectangular shape.

5. Find the area in square feet of the floor of your classroom.

6. Change your answer in exercise 5 to square yards.

Class Activity

▶ **Estimate Volume**

A cube that measures 1 inch on each side is a **cubic inch**. A cubic inch is used to measure volume. Other units that are used to measure volume include a **cubic foot** and a **cubic yard**.

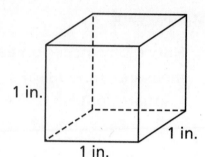

1 in.

1 in.

1 in.

7. How many inches on each side does a cubic foot measure? How many cubic inches are equal to 1 cubic foot?

_____

8. How many feet on each side does a cubic yard measure? How many cubic feet are equal to 1 cubic yard?

_____

Measure volume and show your work.

9. Find the volume in cubic inches of a small object or a small three-dimensional space.

10. Find the volume in cubic feet of your classroom.

11. Change your answer in exercise 10 to cubic yards.

▶ Pounds and Ounces

The pound is the primary unit of weight in our customary system. One **pound** is equal to 16 **ounces**.

Fractions of 1 pound are often used to measure weight. For example, butter and margarine are sold in 1-pound packages that contain four separately wrapped sticks.

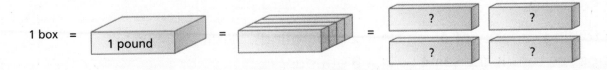

1 box = 1 pound = ? ? ? ?

1. In simplest form, what fraction of 1 pound is one stick?

_____

2. What is the weight in ounces of one stick?

_____

3. In simplest form, what fraction of 1 pound is two sticks?

_____

4. What is the total weight in ounces of two sticks?

_____

5. In simplest form, what fraction of 1 pound is three sticks?

_____

6. What is the total weight in ounces of three sticks?

_____

7. A recipe requires 2 ounces of butter or margarine. How many sticks of butter or margarine should be used in the recipe?

_____

Vocabulary

ton

▶ **Tons**

The weight of heavy items such as cars, trucks, boats, elephants, and whales is measured in **tons**. One ton is equal to 2,000 pounds.

8. The cargo capacity of a small pickup truck is $\frac{1}{2}$ ton. How many pounds of cargo is the same as $\frac{1}{2}$ ton?

_____

9. The towing capacity of a vehicle is 2,500 pounds. What number of tons is the same as 2,500 pounds?

_____

10. A ship weighs 12,450 tons. In pounds, the ship weighs 24,900,000 pounds. Although either weight can be used to describe the ship, the weight that is most often used is 12,450 tons, not 24,900,000 pounds. Why?

_____

_____

_____

_____

11. A container weighs 4 ounces. A shipment of containers weighs 1 ton. How many containers are in the shipment? Show your work.

_____

Convert.

12. $1\frac{1}{2}$ tons = _____ pounds

13. 4,000 pounds = _____ tons

14. 5 tons = _____ pounds

15. 7,000 pounds = _____ tons

16. $\frac{1}{4}$ ton = _____ pounds

17. 6,500 pounds = _____ tons

Weight

Name _____ **Date** _____

Vocabulary	
cup	pint
fluid ounce	gallon
quart	

▶ Units of Capacity

In the customary system, the primary unit of capacity is a **cup**.

1 cup =8 **fluid ounces**   4 cups  =1 **quart**

2 cups =1 **pint**   4 quarts = 1 **gallon**

1. What fraction of 1 cup is 1 fluid ounce?

   _____

2. How many fluid ounces are equal to 1 pint?
   In simplest form, what fraction of 1 pint is 1 cup?

   _____

3. How many fluid ounces are equal to 1 quart?
   In simplest form, what fraction of 1 quart is 1 cup?

   _____

4. How many fluid ounces are equal to 1 gallon?
   In simplest form, what fraction of 1 gallon is 1 cup?

   _____

5. In simplest form, what fraction of 1 gallon is 1 pint?

   _____

6. In simplest form, what fraction of 1 gallon is 1 quart?

   _____

Name _____

Date _____

▶ Solve Capacity Problems

Solve.

Show your work.

7. Alicia adds 4 fluid ounces of grapefruit juice to $\frac{1}{2}$ cup of orange juice. What fraction of 1 cup of juice does she make?

   _____

8. Jay has 1 cup of water. He pours out $\frac{1}{3}$ of the water. To the nearest whole fluid ounce, how many ounces of water remain in the cup?

   _____

9. Sebastian feeds his dog $1\frac{1}{4}$ cups of food each morning, and $1\frac{1}{4}$ cups each evening. How many cups of food does he feed his dog every week?

   _____

10. Five quarts of motor oil are needed when the oil in Tika's car is changed. Tika purchased two new 1-gallon containers of oil, then changed the oil in her car. What amount of new oil did Tika not use?

    _____

11. Each bottle of apple juice contains 12 fluid ounces. A shopper purchased 8 bottles. How many quarts of apple juice did the shopper purchase?

    _____

Convert.

12. 2 fluid ounces = _____ cup

13. 8 cups = _____ quarts

14. 10 quarts = _____ gallons

15. $1\frac{1}{2}$ cups = _____ fluid ounces

16. 12 cups = _____ quarts

17. 5 gallons = _____ cups

Capacity

▶ Fractions of an Hour

1. These clocks all show times after noon (P.M.). What time is shown on each clock?

Clock A   Clock B   Clock C

_____   _____   _____

2. In simplest form, what fraction of 1 hour does the minute hand on Clock A show?

_____

3. Write the time shown on Clock A, using fraction words.

_____

4. Write the times shown on Clocks B and C, using fraction words.

_____

5. How much time has passed from Clock B to Clock C?

_____

6. How much time has passed from Clock B to Clock A?

_____

7. The school bus arrives in $\frac{3}{4}$ of an hour. If the bus is on time, in how many minutes will it arrive?

_____

8. Each day of the week, Molly practices piano for $\frac{1}{3}$ of an hour. How many minutes does she practice each week? How many hours?

Vocabulary

Fahrenheit

▶ Fahrenheit Temperatures

The temperature scale in our customary system is called degrees **Fahrenheit** (°F). Water freezes at 32°F and boils at 212°F.

Answer these questions about temperature.

9. What is a comfortable temperature for the inside of your classroom?

_____

10. Suppose the temperature outside your classroom is 52°F. How will you dress to go outside for recess?

_____

11. How will you dress for recess if the outside temperature is 85°F?

_____

12. The temperature at 6:00 A.M. was 25°F and the temperature at noon was 45°F. During that time, did the temperature increase or decrease? By how many degrees?

_____

13. If the temperature outside is 27°F, is it more likely to be raining or snowing? How do you know?

_____

14. A thermometer placed in the shade of Andy's backyard reads 105°F. Where in the United States might Andy live?

_____

15. The normal temperature for the human body is about 98.6°F. Vanessa's temperature is 102°F. Does she have a fever? How do you know?

_____

250°F
240°
230°
220°
210°
200°
190°
180°
170°
160°
150°
140°
130°
120°
110°
100°
90°
80°
70°
60°
50°
40°
30°
20°
10°
0°

water boils

water freezes

Class Activity

▶ Solve Problems Involving Temperatures

Use the thermometer at the right to solve the following problems.

Farenheit

16. The distance between two consecutive tick marks represents what number of degrees? _____

17. What is the maximum temperature the thermometer can display? What is the minimum temperature it can display? _____

18. The high temperature of the day was 3°F. The low temperature of the day was 4°F lower. What was the low temperature of the day? _____

19. The low temperature of the day was –5°F. The high temperature of the day was 10°F higher. What was the high temperature of the day? _____

20. The 6 A.M. temperature was –7°F. The 6 P.M. temperature was 8°F. How many degrees did the temperature change from 6 A.M. to 6 P.M.?

_____

Was the change an increase or a decrease?

_____

21. The 3 P.M. temperature was 10°F. The 11 p.m. temperature was –2°F. By how many degrees did the temperature change from 3 P.M. to 11 P.M.?

_____

Was the change an increase or a decrease?

_____

Going Further

▶ Negative Numbers on the Number Line

Integers include the set of whole numbers (1, 2, 3, …) and their opposites (–1, –2, –3, …) and 0. The number line below is an integer number line.

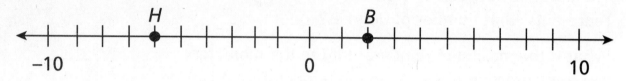

–10 0 10

1. Label each tick mark with the integer it represents.

2. What integer represents the location of point _H_? _____

3. What integer represents the location of point _B_? _____

Plot the following points on the number line.

4. point _R_ at –1   5. point _Y_ at 4   6. point _N_ at –9   7. point _Z_ at 10

Solve.

8. What opposite integers are five units to the left and five units to the right of 0? _____

9. On a number line, an integer is to the right of another integer. Which integer is larger? Explain how you know.

_____

_____

_____

Use the number line at the top of the page to compare these integers. Write >, <, or =.

10. 1 ◯ 9   11. 3 ◯ –2   12. –5 ◯ 6   13. –3 ◯ –10

14. –6 ◯ 6   15. –4 ◯ –4   16. 7 ◯ –7   17. –2 ◯ –1

Name　　　　　　　　　　　　　　　　　　　**Date**

1. How many inches are in 1 yard?

　　　　　　　　　　　　　　　　　

2. Draw a line segment that is $2\frac{3}{4}$ inches long.

3. a. What is the area of this rectangle in square inches?

　　　　　　　　　　　　　　

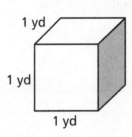

11 in.

17 in.

   b. Is its area greater or less than 1 square foot?

　　　　　　　　　　　　　　

4. How many cubic feet are in one cubic yard?

　　　　　　　　　　　　　　

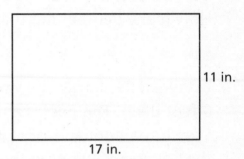

1 yd

1 yd

1 yd

Solve.

5. Justine needs 30 ounces of butter. How many pounds of butter should she buy?

　　　　　　　　　　　　　　

6. A builder is loading a small truck with 20-pound bags of sand. The truck can carry 2 tons. How many bags of sand can it carry?

　　　　　　　　　　　　　　

7. A factory worker needs to pour 8 cups of vanilla into 2-ounce jars. How many jars does the worker need?

8. Each school day, Alvin rides a bus for $\frac{1}{4}$ hour to school and $\frac{1}{4}$ hour home from school. How many minutes does he spend on the bus in a school week? How many hours?

_____

9. On Tuesday, it was 3°F at 8:00 A.M. and 15°F at noon. How many degrees did the temperature rise?

_____

10. **Extended Response** The water in a swimming pool is 6 feet deep. The pool is a rectangle 18 feet by 15 feet. Sketch the pool and label its dimensions in yards. What is the volume of water in the pool in cubic yards? Explain your thinking.

_____

_____

_____

_____

▶ Fractions and Percents

Percent *means per hundred.*

0.25
$\frac{25}{100}$

25% of the pennies means 25 of 100 pennies

$$\frac{25}{100} = \frac{1}{4}$$

Discuss What number of cents do the fractions
$\frac{25}{100}$ of a dollar and $\frac{1}{4}$ of a dollar represent?
Explain why.

Write the missing numerator or denominator or the missing percent.

1. $50\% = \frac{}{100} = \frac{}{2}$

2. $75\% = \frac{}{100} = \frac{3}{}$

3. $20\% = \frac{}{100} = \frac{}{5}$

4. _____ $\% = \frac{60}{100} = \frac{}{5}$

5. _____ $\% = \frac{30}{100} = \frac{}{10}$

6. _____ $\% = \frac{70}{100} = \frac{7}{}$

7. $\frac{3}{4} = \frac{}{100} = $ _____ $\%$

8. $\frac{1}{4} = \frac{}{100} = $ _____ $\%$

9. $\frac{9}{10} = \frac{}{100} = $ _____ $\%$

10. $\frac{1}{2} = \frac{}{100} = $ _____ $\%$

11. $\frac{1}{10} = \frac{}{100} = $ _____ $\%$

12. $\frac{2}{5} = \frac{}{100} = $ _____ $\%$

Solve.

13. Four-fifths of the students in Jim's class are wearing sneakers today. What percent of the students are wearing sneakers today?

_____

14. Ten percent of the vehicles in a parking lot are trucks. If there are 100 vehicles in the parking lot, how many of those vehicles are trucks?

_____

▶ Decimals and Percents

Write the equivalent percent or decimal.

15. 0.25 = _____%

16. 0.75 = _____%

17. 0.50 = _____%

18. _____ = 17%

19. _____ = 8%

20. _____ = 80%

21. 0.42 = _____%

22. 0.03 = _____%

23. 0.7 = _____%

24. _____ = 86%

25. _____ = 4%

26. _____ = 99%

27. 0.3 = _____%

28. _____ = 67%

29. 0.01 = _____%

Solve.

30. During a math discussion, one student said that an equivalent fraction for 5% was $\frac{5}{10}$. Another student said that $\frac{50}{1,000}$ was an equivalent fraction. Was either student correct? Explain why or why not.

_____

_____

_____

31. During a math discussion, a student stated that the whole number 1 is a decimal equivalent for 100%. Is the student correct? Explain why or why not.

_____

_____

Class Activity

▶ Rates and Unit Cost

A **rate** relates two quantities, such as *a* and *b*, usually by division.

We can write this as $a \div b$ or in fraction notation as $\frac{a}{b}$.

A **unit rate** has a divisor of 1. We can write a unit rate without the 1 if we include the word *per*. For example, 60 miles in 1 hour is the same as 60 miles per hour. A unit rate often describes speed or cost.

Solve.

1. Ms. Chu drives 120 miles in 2 hours. Her unit rate is _____ miles per hour. This rate tells the _____
   _____ .

2. The cost of purchasing 3 videos is $15. The unit rate is _____ per video. This rate tells the _____

3. The directions on a can of orange juice read: Mix 4 cans of water with 1 can of concentrate. The unit rate is _____ cans of water per 1 can of concentrate. This rate tells the

   _____

Rewrite each unit rate using the word *per*.

4. 12 months in 1 year   _____

5. 6 pictures on 1 page   _____

6. $10 each week   _____

Solve.

7. The unit cost of one pencil is 39¢. What is the cost of a dozen pencils?

8. What unit rate is represented by a car traveling 325 miles in 5 hours?

_____   _____

▶ Rate Tables

Complete each table. Use the tables to answer the questions.

9.

Unit Rate: $8 per hour	
Number of Hours	Dollars Earned
1	
2	
3	
4	
5	

10.

Unit Rate: 2 slices per person	
Number of People	Slices of Pizza
0	
1	
2	
3	
4	

11. How many hours must Tika baby-sit to earn $48? Use the table in exercise 9. _____

12. Brent ordered 18 slices of pizza. How many people is Brent planning to serve? Use the table in exercise 10. _____

13.

Unit Rate: $3 per gallon							
Gallons of Milk	1	2	3	4	5	6	7
Cost							

14.

Unit Rate: 50 miles per hour (mph)							
Time in Hours	0	2	4	5	6	8	10
Distance in Miles							

15. Is $30 a reasonable estimate of the cost of 10 gallons of milk? Why or why not? Use the table in exercise 13.

_____

16. An 8-ounce jar of peanut butter costs $2.48, and a 20-ounce jar costs $5.40. Which jar costs less per ounce? Explain.

_____

► Ratios

A **ratio** shows how two quantities are related to each other by some situation. Every ratio is written in a particular order, often using a colon (:). When we read a ratio, we say the word *to* when we read the colon. The ratio of 4 cats to 3 dogs is written 4:3 and read, "4 to 3."

1. There are 13 boys and 12 girls in the class.

   What is the ratio of girls to boys? _____

   What is the ratio of boys to girls? _____

2. A right triangle has a base of 9 inches and a height of 5 inches.

   Its ratio of height to base is _____.

   Its ratio of base to height is _____.

3. Davy helps his sister Lynn deliver newspapers every Saturday. Davy earns $3, and Lynn earns $7. Complete the tables below to show how much Davy and Lynn earn by working several weeks.

Linked Multiplication Table

Week	Davy 3	Lynn 7
0	0	0
1		
2		
3		
4		
5		
6		
7		

Ratio Table

	Davy 3	Lynn 7
	0	0
+ 3			+ 7
+ ___			+ ___
+ ___			+ ___
+ ___			+ ___
+ ___			+ ___
+ ___			+ ___
+ ___			+ ___

E–3

Class Activity

Name _____ Date _____

Vocabulary

ratio table

► Ratio Tables

A **ratio table** lists multiples of a ratio. We can think of a ratio table as two columns (or two rows) of a multiplication table. The columns (and the rows) of a ratio table are proportional. Two ratios are proportional if one ratio is a multiple of the other.

Use the information below to complete the tables.

4. Mr. Hall is framing pictures. Each picture has a width to height ratio of 8:5. Complete Table 4 below to show possible widths and heights for Mr. Hall's frames.

5. The second hand of a clock completes 1 revolution every 60 seconds. Complete Table 5 below to show the number of revolutions (*r*) for multiples of 60 seconds (sec).

6. A store is offering prizes. For every 10 customers, 3 prizes are awarded. In the first row of Table 6, write the ratio of customers (*c*) to prizes (*p*). Then complete Table 6.

Table 4

Width : Height

8	5
16	10
24	

Table 5

(*r*)	(sec)
1	60
4	
	480
10	
2	
	720
9	
	180
20	

Table 6

(*c*)	(*p*)
	30
70	
	48
200	
80	
	15
40	
	36

7. Write a ratio questions for each table that your classmates can answer by using the tables.

Ratios

Glossary

acre A measure of land area. An acre is equal to 4,840 square yards.

acute angle An angle smaller than a right angle.

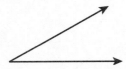

acute triangle A triangle with three acute angles.

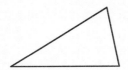

addend One of two or more numbers added together to find a sum.

Example: 7 + 8 = 15

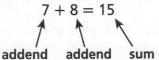

addend   addend   sum

Algebraic Notation Method A strategy based on the Distributive Property in which a factor is decomposed to create simpler algebraic expressions, and the distributive property is applied.

Example: 9 • 28 = 9 • (20 + 8)
= (9 • 20) + (9 • 8)
= 180 + 72
= 252

analog clock A clock with a face and hands.

angle A figure formed by two rays with the same endpoint.

array An arrangement of objects, symbols, or numbers in rows and columns.

area The amount of surface covered or enclosed by a figure measured in square units.

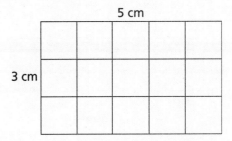

5 cm

3 cm

Associative Property of Addition Grouping the addends in different ways does not change the sum.

Example: 3 + (5 + 7) = 15
(3 + 5) + 7 = 15

Associative Property of Multiplication Grouping the factors in different ways does not change the product.

Example: 3 × (5 × 7) = 105
(3 × 5) × 7 = 105

Glossary (Continued)

average (mean) The size of each of *n* equal groups made from *n* data values. It is calculated by adding the values and dividing by *n*.

Example: 75, 84, 89, 91, 101
   75 + 84 + 89 + 91 + 101 = 440,
   then 440 ÷ 5 = 88. The average is 88.

B

bar graph A graph that uses bars to show data. The bars may be vertical or horizontal.

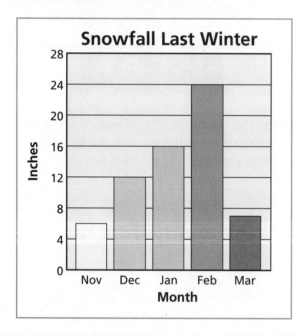

base For a triangle or parallelogram, a base is any side. For a trapezoid, a base is either of the parallel sides. For a prism, a base is one of the congruent parallel faces that may not be rectangular. For a pyramid, the base is the face that does not touch the vertex of the pyramid.

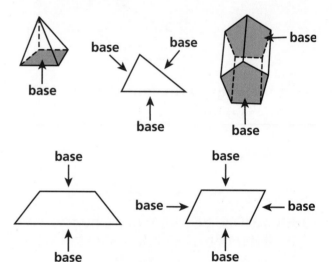

break-apart drawing A diagram that shows two addends and the sum.

C

capacity A measure of how much a container can hold.

Celsius The metric temperature scale.

center The point that is the same distance from every point on the circle.

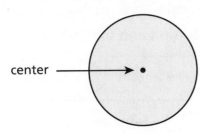

center →

centimeter A unit of measure in the metric system that equals one hundredth of a meter. 1 cm = 0.01 m

change minus A change situation that can be represented by subtraction. In a change minus situation, the starting number, the change, or the result will be unknown.

Example:

Unknown Start	Unknown Change	Unknown Result
$n - 2 = 3$	$5 - n = 3$	$5 - 2 = n$

change plus A change situation that can be represented by addition. In a change plus situation, the starting number, the change, or the result will be unknown.

Example:

Unknown Start	Unknown Change	Unknown Result
$n + 2 = 5$	$3 + n = 5$	$3 + 2 = n$

circle A plane figure that forms a closed path so that all the points on the path are the same distance from a point called the center.

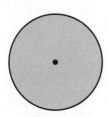

circle graph A graph that uses parts of a circle to show data.

Example:

Favorite Fiction Books

circumference The distance around a circle.

closed Having no endpoints.

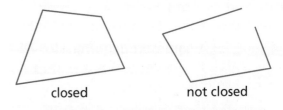

closed   not closed

collection situations Situations that involve putting together (joining) or taking apart (separating) groups.

column A part of a table or array that contains items arranged vertically.

Glossary (Continued)

combination situation A situation in which the number of possible different combinations is determined. A table can sometimes be used to show all possible combinations; multiplication can be used to calculate the number of combinations.

Example:

Different Sandwich Combinations

	peanut butter	cheese	turkey
wheat bread	peanut butter on wheat bread	cheese on wheat bread	turkey on wheat bread
white bread	peanut butter on white bread	cheese on white bread	turkey on white bread

Number of combinations = 3 × 2 = 6

common denominator A common multiple of two or more denominators.

Example: A common denominator of $\frac{1}{2}$ and $\frac{1}{3}$ is 6 because 6 is a multiple of 2 and 3.

Commutative Property of Addition Changing the order of addends does not change the sum.

Example: 3 + 8 = 11
8 + 3 = 11

Commutative Property of Multiplication Changing the order of factors does not change the product.

Example: 3 × 8 = 24
8 × 3 = 24

compare Describe quantities as greater than, less than, or equal to each other.

comparison bars Bars that represent the larger amount and smaller amount in a comparison situation.

For addition and subtraction:

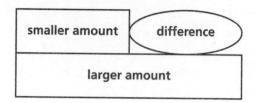

For multiplication and division:

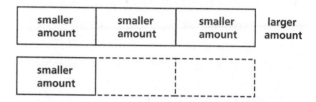

comparison situation A situation in which two amounts are compared by addition or by multiplication. An *additive comparison situation* compares by asking or telling how much more (how much less) one amount is than another. A *multiplicative comparison situation* compares by asking or telling how many times as many one amount is as another. The multiplicative comparison may also be made using fraction language. For example, you can say, "Sally has one fourth as much as Tom has," instead of saying "Tom has 4 times as much as Sally has."

complex figure A figure made by combining simple geometric figures like rectangles and triangles.

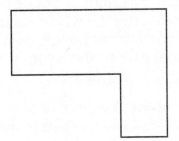

composite number A number greater than 1 that has more than one factor pair. Examples of composite numbers are 10 and 18. The factor pairs of 10 are 1 and 10, 2 and 5. The factor pairs of 18 are 1 and 18, 2 and 9, 3 and 6.

concave A polygon is concave if at least one diagonal is outside of the polygon.

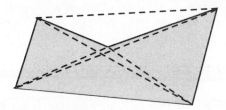

cone A solid figure with a curved base and a single vertex.

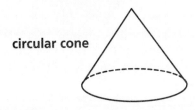

circular cone

congruent Exactly the same size and shape.

Example: Triangles *ABC* and *PQR* are congruent.

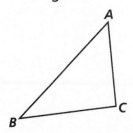

convex A polygon is convex if all of the diagonals are inside the polygon.

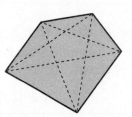

coordinate plane A system of coordinates formed by the perpendicular intersection of horizontal and vertical number lines.

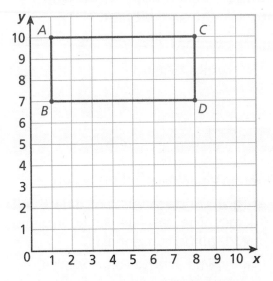

cube A solid figure that has 6 faces that are congruent squares.

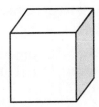

cubic centimeter A metric unit for measuring volume. It is the volume of a cube with one-centimeter edges.

cubic foot A unit for measuring volume. It is the volume of a cube with one-foot edges.

Glossary (Continued)

cubic inch A unit for measuring volume. It is the volume of a cube with one-inch edges.

cubic meter A metric unit for measuring volume. It is the volume of a cube with one-meter edges.

cubic yard A unit for measuring volume. It is the volume of a cube with one-yard edges.

cup A unit of capacity in the customary system that equals 8 ounces.

cylinder A solid figure with two congruent curved bases.

circular cylinder

D

data A collection of information.

categorical data A set of data that is names. The data are sorted into non-overlapping categories.

Example: Favorite color or most popular pet

continuous data A set of data entries that are related to each other. Data accumulate between the points on a line graph because there are values between the points.

Example: Height of a plant over a 5-day period

discrete data Data that have separate, countable values. The data are not related to each other.

Example: Number of students in different classes

numerical data Any set of data that can be described using numbers.

Example: Height of different trees or number of cans on a shelf

decimal number A representation of a number using the numerals 0 to 9, in which each digit has a value 10 times the digit to its right. A dot or **decimal point** separates the whole-number part of the number on the left from the fractional part on the right.

Examples: 1.23 and 0.3

decimal point A symbol used to separate dollars and cents in money amounts or to separate ones and tenths in decimal numbers.

Examples:

$8.59   1.2

decimal point

decimeter A unit of measure in the metric system that equals one tenth of a meter. 1 dm = 0.1 m

denominator The number below the bar in a fraction. It shows the total number of equal parts in the fraction.

Example:

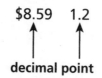

$\frac{3}{4}$ ← denominator

diagonal A line segment that connects vertices of a polygon, but is not a side of the polygon.

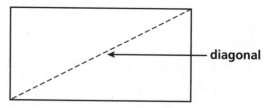

diagonal

diameter A line segment from one side of a circle to the other through the center. Also the length of that segment.

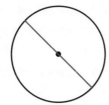

difference The result of a subtraction.

Example: 54 − 37 = 17 ← difference

digit Any of the symbols 0, 1, 2, 3, 4, 5, 6, 7, 8, or 9.

digital clock A clock that shows us the hour and minutes with numbers.

Digit-by-Digit A method used to solve a division problem.

Put in only one digit at a time.

$$
\begin{array}{r}
5 \\
7\overline{)3{,}822} \\
-35 \\
\hline
32
\end{array}
\qquad
\begin{array}{r}
54 \\
7\overline{)3{,}822} \\
-35 \\
\hline
32 \\
-28 \\
\hline
42
\end{array}
\qquad
\begin{array}{r}
546 \\
7\overline{)3{,}822} \\
-35 \\
\hline
32 \\
-28 \\
\hline
42 \\
-42
\end{array}
$$

dimension The height, length, or width.

Examples:

A line segment has only length, so it has *one* dimension.

A rectangle has length and width, so it has *two* dimensions.

A cube has length, width, and height, so it has *three* dimensions.

Distributive Property You can multiply a sum by a number, or multiply each addend by the number and add the products; the result is the same.

Example:

$$3 \times (2 + 4) = (3 \times 2) + (3 \times 4)$$
$$3 \times 6 \quad = \quad 6 \quad + \quad 12$$
$$18 \quad = \quad 18$$

dividend The number that is divided in division.

Example: $9\overline{)63}^{\,7}$, 63 is the dividend.

divisible A number is divisible by another number if the quotient is a whole number with a remainder of 0.

divisor The number you divide by in division.

Example: $9\overline{)63}^{\,7}$, 9 is the divisor.

dot array An arrangement of dots in rows and columns.

double bar graph Data is compared by using pairs of bars drawn next to each other.

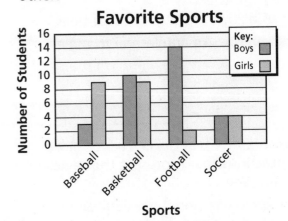

Glossary (Continued)

edge The line segment where two faces of a three-dimensional figure meet.

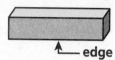
edge

equally likely In probability, equally likely means having the same chance of occurring.

Example: When flipping a coin, the coin is **equally likely** to land on heads or tails.

Equal-Shares Drawing A diagram that shows a number separated into equal parts.

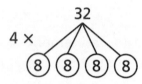

4 × 32
(8) (8) (8) (8)

equation A statement that two expressions are equal. It has an equals sign.

Examples: 32 + 35 = 67
67 = 32 + 34 + 1
(7 × 8) + 1 = 57

equilateral Having all equal sides.

Example: An equilateral triangle

equivalent fractions Two or more fractions that represent the same number.

Example: $\frac{2}{4}$ and $\frac{4}{8}$ are equivalent because they both represent one half.

estimate A number close to an exact amount or to find about how many or how much.

evaluate Substitute a value for a letter (or symbol) and then simplify the expression.

expanded form A way of writing a number that shows the value of each of its digits.

Example: Expanded form of 835:
800 + 30 + 5
8 hundreds + 3 tens + 5 ones

Expanded Notation A method used to solve multiplication and division problems.

Examples:

43 × 67

$$67 = 60 + 7$$
$$\times 43 = 40 + 3$$
$$40 \times 60 = 2400$$
$$40 \times 7 = 280$$
$$3 \times 60 = 180$$
$$3 \times 7 = +21$$
$$2{,}881$$

3,822 ÷ 7

$$\begin{array}{r} 6 \\ 40 \\ 500 \end{array} \Big) 546$$

$$7 \overline{)\, 3{,}822}$$
$$- 3\,500$$
$$\overline{322}$$
$$- 280$$
$$\overline{42}$$
$$- 42$$
$$\overline{0}$$

expression One or more numbers, variables, or numbers and variables with one or more operations.

Examples: 4
$6x$
$6x - 5$
$7 + 4$

face A flat surface of a three-dimensional figure.

factor One of two or more numbers multiplied to find a product.

Example:

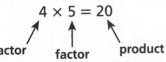

Factor Fireworks Shows how a whole number can be broken down into a product of prime factors.

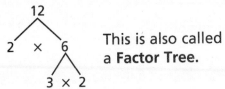

This is also called a **Factor Tree**.

factor pair A factor pair for a number is a pair of whole numbers whose product is that number.

Example: $5 \times 7 = 35$

factor   product
pair

Factor Triangle A diagram that shows a factor pair and the product.

Example: 32
          ÷ / \ ÷
          4 × 8

Fahrenheit The temperature scale used in the United States.

Fast Array A numerical form of an array that shows an unknown factor or unknown product.

4
o o o o
6   o
    o   24
    o
    o
    o

   8
o────────
3 o 24
  o

fluid ounce A unit of capacity in the customary system that equals $\frac{1}{8}$ cup or 2 tablespoons.

foot A U.S. customary unit of length equal to 12 inches.

fraction A number that is the sum of unit fractions, each an equal part of a set or part of a whole.

Examples: $\frac{3}{4} = \frac{1}{4} + \frac{1}{4} + \frac{1}{4}$

$\frac{5}{4} = \frac{1}{4} + \frac{1}{4} + \frac{1}{4} + \frac{1}{4} + \frac{1}{4}$

frequency table A table that shows how many times each event, item, or category occurs.

Frequency Table	
Height	Frequency
47	1
48	2
49	4
50	3
51	1
52	0
53	2
Total	13

function A set of ordered pairs of numbers such that for every first number there is only one possible second number.

Example: The relationship between yards and feet.

Yards	1	2	3	4	5	6	7
Feet	3	6	9	12	15	18	21

function rule A rule that describes the relationship between ordered pairs. It is generally written as an equation. For 3 feet = 1 yard the equation is $3f = y$.

Glossary (Continued)

function table A table of ordered pairs that shows a function.

Rule: add 2	
Input	Output
1	3
2	4
3	5
4	6

Heads	1	2	3	4
Legs	2	4	6	8

G

gallon A unit of capacity in the customary system that equals 4 quarts.

gram The basic unit of mass in the metric system.

greater than (>) A symbol used to compare two numbers. The greater number is given first below.

Example: 33 > 17

33 is greater than 17.

greatest Largest. Used to order three or more quantities or numbers.

H

height The perpendicular distance from a base of a figure to the highest point.

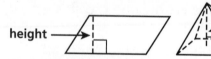

horizontal bar graph A bar graph with horizontal bars.

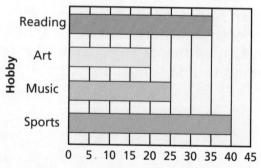

Favorite Hobbies of Lakeview School Fourth-Graders

hundredth A unit fraction representing one of one hundred parts, written as 0.01 or $\frac{1}{100}$.

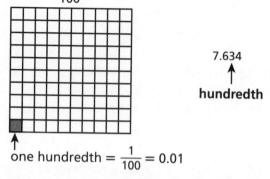

7.634
↑
hundredth

one hundredth = $\frac{1}{100}$ = 0.01

I

Identity Property of Multiplication The product of 1 and any number equals that number.

Example: $10 \times 1 = 10$

improper fraction A fraction that is greater than or equal to 1. The numerator is greater than or equal to the denominator.

Examples: $\frac{13}{4}$ or $\frac{4}{4}$

inch A U.S. customary unit of length.

Example: |—————|
1 inch

inequality A statement that two expressions are not equal.

Examples: $2 < 5$
$4 + 5 > 12 - 8$

integer The set of integers includes the set of positive whole numbers (1, 2, 3, ...) and their opposites (−1, −2, −3, ...) and 0.

inverse operations Opposite or reverse operations that undo each other. Addition and subtraction are inverse operations. Multiplication and division are inverse operations.

Examples: $4 + 6 = 10$ so, $10 - 6 = 4$ and $10 - 4 = 6$.
$3 \times 9 = 27$ so, $27 \div 9 = 3$ and $27 \div 3 = 9$.

isosceles trapezoid A trapezoid with a pair of opposite congruent sides.

isosceles triangle A triangle with at least two congruent sides.

K

kilogram A unit of mass in the metric system that equals one thousand grams. 1 kg = 1,000 g

kiloliter A unit of capacity in the metric system that equals one thousand liters. 1 kL = 1,000 L

kilometer A unit of length in the metric system that equals 1,000 meters. 1 km = 1,000 m

L

leading language A comparison sentence containing language that suggests which operation to use to solve a problem.

least Smallest. Used to order three or more quantities or numbers.

least common denominator The least common multiple of two or more denominators.

Example: The least common denominator of $\frac{1}{2}$ and $\frac{1}{3}$ is 6 because 6 is the smallest multiple of 2 and 3.

length The measure of a line segment or one side or edge of a figure.

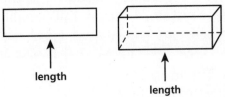

less than (<) A symbol used to compare two numbers. The smaller number is given first below.

Example: $54 < 78$
54 is less than 78.

line A straight path that goes on forever in opposite directions.

Example: line *AB*

line of symmetry A line that divides a figure into two congruent parts.

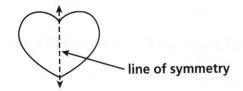

line plot A diagram that shows the frequency of data on a number line.

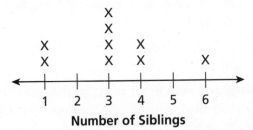

Number of Siblings

line segment Part of a line that has two endpoints.

Glossary (Continued)

line symmetry A figure has line symmetry if it can be folded along a line to create two halves that match exactly.

liter The basic unit of capacity in the metric system. 1 liter = 1,000 milliliters

M

mass The measure of the amount of matter in an object.

mean (average) The size of each of n equal groups made from n data values. It is calculated by adding the values and dividing by n.

Examples: 75, 84, 89, 91, 101
$75 + 84 + 89 + 91 + 101 = 440$,
then $440 \div 5 = 88$. The mean is **88**.

measure of central tendency The mean, median, or mode of a set of numbers.

median The middle number in a set of ordered numbers. For an even number of numbers, the median is the average of the two middle numbers.

Examples: 13 26 34 47 52
The median for this set is **34**.
8 8 12 14 20 21
The median for this set is
$(12 + 14) \div 2 = 13$.

meter The basic unit of length in the metric system.

mile A U.S. customary unit of length equal to 5,280 feet.

milligram A unit of mass in the metric system that equals one thousandth of a gram. 1 mg = 0.001 g

milliliter A unit of capacity in the metric system that equals one thousandth of a liter. 1 mL = 0.001 L

millimeter A unit of length in the metric system that equals one thousandth of a meter. 1 mm = 0.001 m

misleading language Language in a comparing sentence that may cause you to do the wrong operation.

Example: John's age is 3 *more than* Jessica's. If John is 12, how old is Jessica?

mixed number A number that can be represented by a whole number and a fraction.

Example: $4\frac{1}{2} = 4 + \frac{1}{2}$

mode The number that appears most frequently in a set of numbers.

Example: 2, 4, 4, 4, 5, 7, 7
4 is the mode in this set of numbers.

multiple A number that is the product of a given number and any whole number.

Examples: $4 \times 1 = 4$, so 4 is a multiple of 4.
$4 \times 2 = 8$, so 8 is a multiple of 4.

N

net A flat pattern that can be folded to make a solid figure.

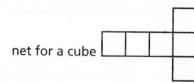

net for a cube

number line A line that extends, without end, in each direction and shows numbers as a series of points. The location of each number is shown by its distance from 0.

number sentence A mathematical statement that uses =, <, or > to show how numbers or expressions are related. The types of number sentences are equations and inequalities.

Example: $25 + 25 = 50$
$13 > 8 + 2$

numerator The number above the bar in a fraction. It shows the number of equal parts.

Example:

$\frac{3}{4}$ ← numerator $\quad \frac{3}{4} = \frac{1}{4} + \frac{1}{4} + \frac{1}{4}$

O

obtuse angle An angle greater than a right angle and less than a straight angle.

obtuse triangle A triangle with one obtuse angle.

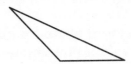

Order of Operations A set of rules that state the order in which operations should be done.

STEPS: -Compute inside parentheses first.
      -Multiply and divide from left to right.
      -Add and subtract from left to right.

ordered pair A pair of numbers that shows the position of a point on a coordinate grid.

Example: The ordered pair (3, 4) represents a point 3 units to the right of the y-axis and 4 units above the x-axis.

origin The point (0, 0) on a two-dimensional coordinate grid.

ounce A unit of weight equal to one sixteenth of a pound. A unit of capacity equal to one eighth of a cup (also called a fluid ounce).

P

parallel Lines in the same plane that never intersect are parallel. Line segments and rays that are part of parallel lines are also parallel.

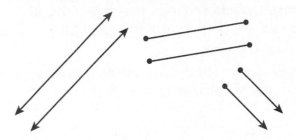

parallelogram A quadrilateral with both pairs of opposite sides parallel.

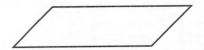

Partial-Quotients Method A method used to solve division problems where the partial quotients are written next to the division problem instead of above it.

Example:
$$
\begin{array}{r}
8\overline{)178} \\
-160 \quad | \; 20 \\
\hline
18 \\
-16 \quad | \; 2 \\
\hline
2 \quad | \; 22 \\
\hline
22 \;\; R2
\end{array}
$$

pattern A sequence that can be described by a rule.

pentagon A polygon with five sides.

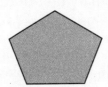

Glossary (Continued)

percent Percent means per hundred or out of a hundred.

Example: 50% can be written as $\frac{50}{100}$ or 0.50.

perimeter The distance around a figure.

perpendicular Lines, line segments, or rays are perpendicular if they form right angles.

Example: These two line segments are perpendicular.

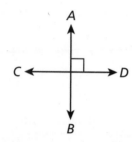

pi A special number equal to the circumference of a circle divided by its diameter. Pi can be represented by the symbol π and is approximately 3.14.

pictograph A graph that uses pictures or symbols to represent data.

Books Checked Out of Library	
Student	
Najee	📖📖
Tariq	📖📖📖📖📖📖
Celine	📖📖📖📖📖📖📖📖
Jamarcus	📖📖📖
Brooke	📖📖📖📖

📖 = 5 books

pint A customary unit of capacity that equals 16 fluid ounces or $\frac{1}{2}$ quart.

place value The value assigned to the place that a digit occupies in a number.

Example: 235

The 2 is in the hundreds place, so its value is 200.

place-value drawing A drawing that represents a number. Thousands are represented by vertical rectangles, hundreds are represented by squares, tens are represented by vertical lines, and ones by small circles.

Example:

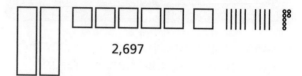

2,697

place-value form A way of writing a number that uses digits and place value names.

Example: 8 thousands 5 hundreds 6 tens 2 ones

plane A flat surface that extends without end.

polygon A closed plane figure with sides made of straight line segments.

pound A unit of weight in the U.S. customary system.

prime number A number greater than 1 that has 1 and itself as the only factor pair. Examples of prime numbers are 2, 7, and 13. The only factor pair of 7 is 1 and 7.

prism A solid figure with two congruent parallel bases joined by rectangular faces. Prisms are named by the shape of their bases.

pentagonal prism

probability A number between 0 and 1 that represents the chance of an event happening.

product The answer to a multiplication problem.

Example: $9 \times 7 = 63$

product

protractor A semicircular tool for measuring and constructing angles.

pyramid A solid with a polygon for a base whose faces meet at a point called the vertex.

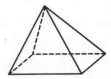

Q

quadrilateral A polygon with four sides.

quart A customary unit of capacity that equals 32 ounces or 4 cups.

quotient The answer to a division problem.

Example: $9\overline{)63}$; 7 is the quotient.

R

radius A line segment that connects the center of a circle to any point on that circle. Also the length of that line segment.

range The difference between the greatest number and the least number in a set.

rate A rate shows how two quantities that have different units are related to each other, usually by using division.

ratio A ratio shows how two quantities are related to each other, usually by using division.

ratio table A table with two columns that lists multiples of a ratio.

ray Part of a line that has one endpoint and extends without end in one direction.

rectangle A parallelogram with four right angles.

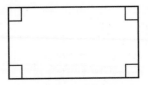

Rectangle Sections A method using rectangle drawings to solve multiplication or division problems.

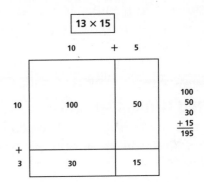

a.

b.   c.

d.   e.   f.

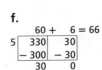

Glossary (Continued)

reflection A transformation that flips a figure onto a congruent image. Sometimes called a *flip*.

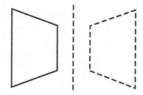

regular polygon Having all sides and angles congruent.

Example: A square is a regular quadrilateral.

remainder The number left over after dividing two numbers that are not evenly divisible.

Example: $5\overline{)43}$ 8 R3 The remainder is 3.

Repeated Groups situation A multiplication situation in which all groups have the same number of objects.

rhombus A parallelogram with congruent sides.

right angle One of four congruent angles made by perpendicular lines.

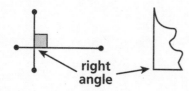

right angle

right triangle A triangle with one right angle.

rotation A turn. A transformation that turns a figure so each point stays an equal distance from a single point.

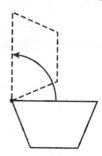

round To find the nearest ten, hundred, thousand, or some other place value. The usual rounding rule is to round up if the next digit to the right is 5 or more and round down if the next digit to the right is less than 5.

Examples: 463 rounded to the nearest ten is 460.
463 rounded to the nearest hundred is 500.

row A part of a table or array that contains items arranged horizontally.

S

scalene A triangle with no equal sides is a scalene triangle.

sequence A set of objects or numbers arranged in a specific order.

Short-Cut Method A strategy for multiplying. It is the current common method in the United States.

Step1	Step2
$\overset{7}{28}$	$\overset{7}{28}$
$\times\ 9$	$\times\ 9$
$\overline{2}$	$\overline{252}$

similar Figures that have the same shape but not necessarily the same size.

simplest form A fraction is in simplest form if there is no whole number (other than 1) that divides evenly into the numerator and denominator.

Examples: $\frac{3}{4}$ This fraction is in simplest form because no number divides evenly into 3 and 4.

simplify an expression Combine like terms and perform operations until all terms have been combined.

simplify a fraction To divide the numerator and the denominator of a fraction by the same number to make an equivalent fraction made from fewer but larger unit fractions.

Example: $\frac{5}{10} = \frac{5 \div 5}{10 \div 5} = \frac{1}{2}$

situation equation An equation that shows the action or the relationship in a problem.

Example: $35 + n = 40$

slant height The height of a triangular face of a pyramid.

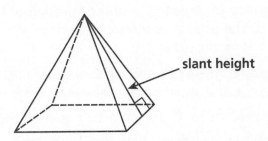

slant height

solution equation An equation that shows the operation to perform in order to solve the problem.

Example: $n = 40 - 35$

sphere A solid figure shaped like a ball.

square A rectangle with 4 congruent sides and 4 right angles. It is also a rhombus.

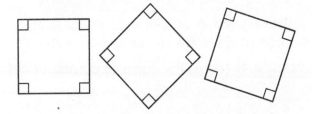

square array An array in which the number of rows equals the number of columns.

square centimeter A unit of area equal to the area of a square with one-centimeter sides.

square decimeter A unit of area equal to the area of a square with one-decimeter sides.

square foot A unit of area equal to the area of a square with one-foot sides.

Glossary (Continued)

square inch A unit of area equal to the area of a square with one-inch sides.

square kilometer A unit of area equal to the area of a square with one-kilometer sides.

square meter A unit of area equal to the area of a square with one-meter sides.

square mile A unit of area equal to the area of a square with one-mile sides.

square millimeter A unit of area equal to the area of a square with one-millimeter sides.

square number The product of a whole number and itself.

Example: $3 \times 3 = 9$

9 is a square number.

square unit A unit of area equal to the area of a square with one-unit sides.

square yard A unit of area equal to the area of a square with one-yard sides.

standard form The form of a number written using digits.

Example: 2,145

stem-and-leaf plot A frequency display that uses place value to organize a set of data.

Central College Team Points Scored	
Stem	Leaf
5	5
6	
7	0 3 4 5
8	0 1 1 2 2 2 4 5 6 6 8
9	1 2 7 8

9 | 2 means 92

sum The answer when adding two or more addends.

Example:

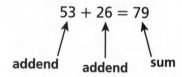

surface area The total area of the two-dimensional surfaces of a three-dimensional figure.

T

table Data arranged in rows and columns.

tally chart A chart that uses tally marks to record and organize data.

Tally Chart	
Height (inches)	Tally
47	///
48	ⵁⵁⵁⵁⵁ
49	//
50	
51	ⵁⵁⵁⵁⵁ /
52	////
53	//

/ is 1

ⵁⵁⵁⵁⵁ is 5

tenth A unit fraction representing one of ten equal parts of a whole, written as 0.1 or $\frac{1}{10}$.

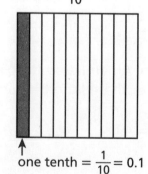

one tenth = $\frac{1}{10}$ = 0.1

term in a pattern A number, a letter, a shape, or an object in a pattern.

term in an expression A number, variable, product, or quotient in an expression. Each term is separated by an operation sign (+ , −).

Example: $3n + 5$ has two terms, $3n$ and 5.

tessellation One or more congruent figures arranged to form a repeating pattern that covers a surface with no gaps or overlaps.

thousandth A unit fraction representing one of one thousand equal parts of a whole, written as 0.001 or $\frac{1}{1,000}$.

ton A unit of weight that equals 2,000 pounds.

tonne A metric unit of mass that equals 1,000 kilograms.

total Sum. The result of addition.

Example: $53 + 26 = 79$

addend addend total (sum)

transformation A change in the position of a figure. Reflections, rotations, and translations are examples of transformations.

translation A transformation that moves a figure along a straight line without turning or flipping. Sometimes called a *slide*.

trapezoid A quadrilateral with one pair of parallel sides.

triangle A polygon with three sides.

triangular prism A prism with two parallel opposite bases that are congruent triangles.

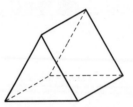

U

unit A standard of measurement.

Examples: Centimeters, pounds, inches, and so on.

unit fraction A fraction whose numerator is 1. It shows one equal part of a whole.

Example: $\frac{1}{4}$

unit rate A rate with a divisor of 1.

Example: 60 miles in 1 hour or 60 miles per hour

V

vertex A point that is shared by two sides of an angle, two sides of a polygon, or edges of a solid figure.

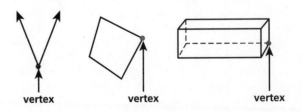

vertex   vertex   vertex

Glossary (Continued)

vertical bar graph A bar graph with vertical bars.

Monday's DVD Rentals at MovieLand

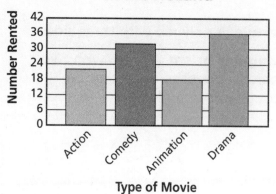

volume The number of cubic units of space occupied by a solid figure.

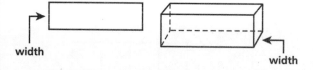

W

width The measure of one side or edge of a figure.

width   width

word form The form of a number written using words instead of digits.

Example: Six hundred thirty-nine

Y

yard A U.S. customary unit of length equal to 3 feet.